STARTING A SUCCESSFUL
SMALL BUSINESS

STARTING A
SUCCESSFUL
SMALL BUSINESS

SECOND EDITION

M J MORRIS

KOGAN
PAGE

Acknowledgements

I must thank my colleagues who gave freely of their time to offer candid, constructive criticism of the draft of the first edition.

Thanks are due to my wife Carole and daughter Eleanor for their considerable help and patience.

In fairness to all it should be said that responsibility for any errors of omission or commission falls entirely on me.

Michael Morris
October 1988

First published in Great Britain in 1985 by
Kogan Page Limited, 120 Pentonville Road,
London N1 9JN.
Second edition 1989.

British Library Cataloguing in Publication Data

Morris, M.J. (Michael John)
    Starting a successful small business. – 2nd
    ed.
    1. Great Britain. Small firms. Organisation.
    – Manuals
    I. Title
    658′.022′0941

    ISBN 1–85091–767–1
    ISBN 1–85091–768–X pbk

Typeset by DP Photosetting, Aylesbury, Bucks
Printed and bound in Great Britain by
Biddles Ltd, Guildford

Contents

CONTENTS

What this Book is for

The aims of this book are simple: to help you to get into business properly, to help you to survive in business, and to explain it all simply and clearly.

Of all the new businesses that are formed – and there are over 100 a week – one in three fails inside a year, and an astonishing four out of five collapse before their fifth birthday. Perhaps the biggest tragedy is that nearly all of them could have been saved by proper preparation, a bit of forward planning, a little more knowledge and a bit less wishful thinking. If their founders had only applied the knowledge that is available more or less for the asking, some would not have gone ahead but most would still be around today.

Going into business can look simple. You think up an idea, get some orders, make the goods, deliver them and get paid. In a very general sense that is all there is to it. But most of the people who fail make one very big mistake. They think that they don't need to do much more, and that any problems can be sorted out as they arise. Some seat-of-the-pants operators do survive, of course, but many more bitterly regret not foreseeing the problems they went on to give themselves.

This book looks at the questions that any new business must deal with, and shows down-to-earth ways of tackling them. My main motive in writing it was straightforward: to make some contribution to cutting down the frightful rate of failure among new firms and all the human misery that goes with it, seeing in its place more real success stories and the happy faces that go with them.

A word of good cheer. Whether it is polar exploration, dentistry on tigers or starting a business the people who tend to survive the experience are those who take the trouble to find out what they are going into. By doing this vital background reading you will learn where the main pitfalls are and how to avoid them.

Who is this book written for? People who plan to make things, mend, sell, service, install or build things are its main audience. It does not deal with shopkeeping of the grocery store variety. A service business may operate from a shop, of course, because it needs a counter for taking in work and a display area for selling parts and reconditioned goods. But it is not a shop first and foremost, so this book *was* written for the person who plans to set it up, as well as all those people making everything from computer hardware to soft toys.

Finally, sex. Or rather, gender. Throughout I have referred to 'he' and the 'businessman'. This is not prejudice, but for ease of reading and economy. 'She' and 'businesswoman' are longer, and 'he or she' and 'businessman or woman' are clumsier too. I hope no one will be offended, because what the book says is applicable to any small firm, whoever is running it.

Whatever your chosen line of business, I do wish you the very best of luck and the achievement of your ambitions.

Michael Morris

Section 1

Introduction and First Steps

1.1 Aims of this section

Before you actually decide to start a business you might give some thought to the demands it will make on you and those around you. A businessman needs certain personal qualities. Your financial position will be different from that of an employee. These topics are explored, and this section aims to give a picture of what is involved in working for yourself, then ends by taking a look at franchising.

1.2 What's running a small firm like?

The first and most obvious differences are having no boss to tell you what to do, and no pay-packet at the end of the week. That excites some people and frightens others. Either way, self-employed people often say that being solely responsible for their income clears their minds wonderfully. As the owner of the business, only you know what absolutely must be done, and what can be left for another day. Only you know that you have to push ahead relentlessly with the job in hand. And only you will deserve the credit for your firm's successes, and the odium for the mistakes. So far, nice and simple. The trouble starts when you realise just how many interruptions a boss gets.

Part of the art of management – and a vital part – is cutting out the trivial, freeing time to give proper attention to the small proportion of matters that is really important. But even that proportion is a large number, and takes a lot of time. To see just how little time people do spend on important things, try keeping a *time log*: over a period of a week you note down on a pad every single thing that you do and for how long. At the end of the week divide them into three categories:

- Items that directly work towards your aims
- Other things that really must be done, but don't mean progress
- Matters that were not really necessary.

Now add up the total time spent on each category. Most people simply do not believe their own figures!

In your business you will be a bit like a middle-distance runner who

13

plans and programmes his race only to find that obstacles keep on cropping up and stopping him. In a small firm there is only one person who makes things happen or holds things up – the boss. If you are bogged down in dealing with some official, your one-man firm just stops work. The official has all the time in the world to get absolutely everything right. And he likes getting out of the office, meeting people and learning about their work. You, by contrast, cannot wait to get rid of him and know you must not let the meeting drag on. Then, when you have escaped and got back to work, the phone rings four times in 15 minutes with other matters needing your urgent attention. Before you realise it, the clock says 5.45 and it is too late to make those pressing calls to people you have to ring back. Now tomorrow morning will be a mess because you will have to chase around town picking up the parts you meant to order this afternoon ... and so it goes on.

It is that kind of don't-know-which-way-to-turn pressure that you need to learn how to cope with. There are always more things clamouring to be done than you can possibly do. When things are quiet it is not much better, for then you get the help-me-I-am-going-broke feeling. When things go well and your plans work out it can be the most rewarding feeling in the world. But you can pay a high price for those rewards, and some people pay the price but are never rewarded.

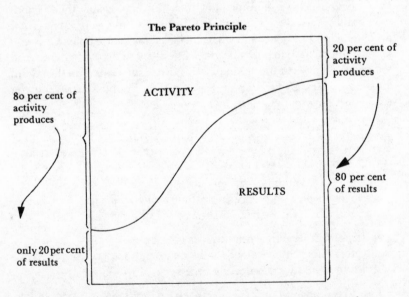

The Pareto Principle

20 per cent of activity produces

80 per cent of activity produces

ACTIVITY

RESULTS

80 per cent of results

only 20 per cent of results

This tells us that some of your time is more or less wasted, but a precious 20 per cent of your efforts produces 80 per cent of your results. The trick is to find that 20 per cent and expand it.

1.3 The demands on you and yours

If you have the sort of job that involves hard work, long hours, and lots of uncertainty, you begin to get some idea of what being the boss is like. As an employee you might not have had to understand the jobs done by people in other departments of firms you have worked for. As your own boss you will need to understand them well enough to do most of those jobs yourself. You probably could bumble along for some time without broadening your horizons, but sooner or later you will hit a snag that will be expensive to overcome or even fatal. In any case, this book is not about that way of doing things.

Just as ignorance of the law is no excuse, so it is inexcusable in a businessman not to understand the basic tools of business – accounts, for example. Thus you need to have the sort of mind that can pick up new knowledge reasonably quickly, and be able to make yourself understood clearly. Being able to get your own way pleasantly is a big help. Not being taken in by appearances is an essential characteristic.

And what of your family? Apart from the strain of living with such a superman, they will also have to get used to seeing very little of you, to having their few outings and treats cancelled at short notice, and, in the early years at least, to a permanent shortage of cash. However keen your spouse is to see you make a go of the business, he or she will have to be superhuman too not to feel jealous at times. You spend all your free time at work, you cancel holidays, you plough all the spare cash back, you talk of nothing else – the business always comes first, and the family last. It is only fair to your family and yourself to warn them about the monster you are bringing into all your lives. The monster may even put the family home at risk (see section 4 on borrowing money), so everyone has a stake in your decision. If the whole family feels the risks are worth taking for the sort of opportunity you have, or if they compare well with the awful alternative, so be it. Family backing is important, for if you do not have it and you mess things up, the effects on your most precious relationships could be dire. Indeed, these extra stresses have been the last straw in many a tottering marriage. If the family is inclined to see only the dark side of things, one or two facts might help them to be more positive. For instance, some of the most successful businessmen in any country are immigrants who often do not even speak the local language at first. Despite this handicap, they build businesses, sometimes on an international scale. Many self-made men never passed an exam in their lives. Their driving force was a simple but original idea, determination to succeed, and the ability to bounce back when things go wrong. Some even failed completely before hitting the jackpot. The late Lord Thomson of Fleet, formerly Roy Thomson, went broke several times in his native Canada before going on to own *The Times*, *The Sunday Times*, Scottish Television and the odd North Sea oil well.

1.4 Sports and pastimes

You should take care to maintain the most important machine in the firm, your body. You need to keep reasonably fit to take the strains placed on you. No need to run a marathon, or to run at all, but eat and drink sensibly, take frequent, moderate exercise and get the sleep you need. Try not to give up all outside interests despite the pressure on your time, so as to give yourself a change and a break. If you play golf off a low handicap, prepare to see your handicap rise. You will not have the time to keep it down. And angling, or any other time-consuming sport, may have to go. One reason for the popularity of squash among business people is that it gets the week's ration of sport over very quickly. But swimming, cycling and walking are probably kinder to your body.

1.5 What sort of person are you?

Most readers may by now be asking themselves if they really have got what it takes to start a firm. So here is a little quiz, to see how you measure up. The idea is to test how you see yourself, and then quite separately to get someone else to mark you. The other person needs to know you quite well, to be relied on to be mercilessly honest, and should therefore probably not be a close relative. The items in the lists are in no particular order. As far as possible they should be related to how you perform at work or in other organisations you may belong to. They might be the TA, a political party, a PTA or just the crowd you go camping with. The important thing is to see how you perform when tasks need doing and decisions have to be made. So someone who knows you just from the pub would probably not be much help.

A. *You ought to score high on most of these:*
- Getting your own way when you want to, without offending too many people
- Spotting potential snags and problems, and getting round them
- Revealing your feelings only when you mean to
- Having a fairly quick mind
- Getting your message across
- Being technically competent to the necessary level
- Seeing opportunities for improvement
- Leading rather than being led
- Not being put off by setbacks

- Having good general health
- Being prepared to have a go
- Will to succeed.

B. *Optional extras that can help a lot:*
- Family support
- Management experience
- Experience of getting things done to tight deadlines
- Skill with figures
- Problem-solving skills
- Experience of persuading people in your work
- Being used to getting many things done at once
- Family background in business
- Experience in your chosen field of business
- Highly priced, scarce, specialised skills
- Lots of money.

Overall these lists are meant to give a picture of the main characteristics of many successful businessmen. They are not comprehensive, as some industries have very specialised requirements. The balance between the items is different for everyone, and there is no one standard success formula, thank heaven. What can be said for certain is that a shrinking violet who never gets his own way or has a new idea, and is a bit slow on the uptake will have a hard time establishing a business. So think carefully and long, and listen to the advice of honest people who know you well, before taking the plunge.

1.6 Four types of people who start businesses

The craftsman
Many businesses are started by people who know how to make things. They are often – but not always – good at it, possessing some highly marketable skills which other people are eager to buy.

The problems that they face usually fall into the following categories:

- Poor salesmanship, so that they fail to convince customers that the full asking price should be paid
- Not realising how valuable their output is, and charging too little
- Assuming that they are forced to go into manufacturing, whereas it might not be necessary: someone else might take that on
- Poor appreciation of what customers really need, as opposed to what they *say* they want

- Indulging their desire to make things to high standards, whether or not that is what people really want
- Having an inflated idea of how special their product is
- Assuming that what they like to make is what customers want to buy
- Treating selling and salesmanship as something that can be looked at only if there is time left after the important process of manufacturing.

If it were possible, one of the most useful experiences they could have would be to work on a 'spieler's' market stall for a few weeks. They would quickly see how a little imagination can re-present a mundane product as something special, which raises the price that people are prepared to pay and their eagerness to buy it. They would learn about the importance of communicating the advantages of a product clearly and in terms that the customers have no trouble in understanding. The lesson would also teach them how to spot winning products quickly and to readjust losers to get them sold. Not everything they saw would be immediately applicable to their own businesses but the attitude of mind would rub off. That attitude tells them that:

- The offering needs to stand out from the crowd
- The same product can be offered in many different ways
- People are attracted by special offers
- Enthusiasm is attractive and convincing
- Offers are often more important than products
- Offers should be unique, or at least seem to be
- Cost of production is rarely related to what people will happily pay
- Successful salesmen steer the interview along a predetermined course
- Asking customers questions keeps them involved in the sales story
- People feel reassured when they buy from a busy seller
- Attractive display and presentation are very important
- Customers expect the salesman to ask for an order – he shouldn't disappoint them.

This does not mean that sales presentations need to verge on showbiz, like those of the more colourful street traders, but modesty, expecting the product's quality to speak for itself, and a lack of pushiness will more or less guarantee perpetual problems and possibly cause failure.

Should the craftsman decide to run his firm as a partnership, his most useful partner will be a salesman. He should avoid getting together with anyone of a meticulous turn of mind: most craftsmen can themselves supply all the worry about detail that a small firm can take. He needs someone with big ideas and a vision that extends beyond the workshop. He needs to be aware that salesmen can be overbearing: their skill is to be good at getting their own way, and the good ones can employ the entire range of legitimate methods of persuasion.

The experienced manager

People with years of management experience behind them who decide to start their own firms often come unstuck. Why? Because many of them think that experience and attitudes from big business can apply anywhere. Some do not realise, until it is too late, that *running a small firm is different.*

What are the most common mistakes? They seem to stem partly from the scale, momentum (and inertia) of the big firm, partly from the special outlook that a manager must have in a large company if he is to survive. For example, in big business it can sometimes be dangerous to admit to not knowing, so people develop techniques to help them bluff their way past danger and to cover up ignorance. When someone starts his own business nobody expects perfection in all departments right from the beginning, and many of the people best able to help will be put off by a know-all attitude. And a lot of very competent advisers are available, and should be used to help in the transition from functional specialist to general manager.

Thus the key challenge is that of converting from a big-company set of attitudes to one better suited to survival as a small-firm owner. The checklist on page 20 shows the main points to watch for. Your experience is valuable, make no mistake, but on its own it does not make you a small-business superman. Most people in bigger organisations have to specialise to a greater or lesser extent. When a manager sets up his own firm he must change into an all-rounder as fast as possible, preferably overnight. His best attributes may be know-how, confidence and competence, and his enemy over-confidence.

Most small firms are founded by people who have worked in small businesses, and have seen their operations close to. This may be why many fail: it can look easier than it is, and not all small businesses have habits that should be copied. Such people do have a head start in many ways, through having seen at least something of how small firms work. Big business experience has been the foundation of many a small-firm success, but only if the special outlook that it encourages is radically altered to meet this completely new challenge.

The salesman

Sales people who start businesses have obvious strengths. That is, if they really do know about selling. Some salesmen are employed to do little

Activity	Big company	Small business
Collecting money from customers	Someone else's job (unless you are the credit manager)	Your job, and crucial to survival
Return on investments	Often expect to postpone profit for a year or two, as long as there will be a return eventually	Has to be more or less immediate
Overall management of the firm	The job of some remote figure	Your main job
Attention to a narrow specialism	You are paid to be a specialist	You are a *general* manager now, so keep the specialism in its place
Break-even point	Often at a high level of sales	Needs to be kept as low as possible
Profit margins	Preferably fat, but volume makes up for thin ones	Must be high, because there is little opportunity to go for volume
Raising money	Usually the job of someone else, on behalf of a firm that carries real weight	Your job, backed up by little or no clout
Attention to detail	It pays to have three people working on something affecting 1 per cent of £100 m sales	Deal only with important things. 1 per cent of your sales is less than £500, most likely
Spending 'small' sums of money	£1,000, £2000 or even £10,000	Spend nothing, if possible; if not, spend little
Using specialist advisers	On the staff, available free and more or less on demand	Select good ones, be prepared to pay, use wisely and get value for money
Prestige and appearances	Big offices and cars, good furniture are vital	Get nothing that doesn't really work hard for you
Delegation and help	People on hand to take on tasks	You do it or it doesn't get done
Complete understanding of objectives	A few people at the top, with big problems of communicating them more widely	Possible for every employee to have it
Responsibility for going broke	Shareholders and directors	You

This is only a selection of some of the main differences between running a small firm and working for a big one. Not all large companies have the slightly muddled attitudes that may be suggested, by any means. But, despite the shake-out of the 1980s, many still do. The table does show the considerable change in attitude that the big-firm manager must undergo if he is to adjust successfully, build on his strengths, and survive.

more than take orders, or are employed in a narrow field and cannot apply the general principles of selling elsewhere. Most, however, have a good idea of what makes people tick, and how to get orders from customers. If they have worked for really lively companies they will also have been exposed to many different sales-promotional techniques. Their strength will be exactly what is lacked by the craftsman discussed earlier.

But, like everyone, many a salesman has his weaknesses which include:

- Over-confidence in his own judgement
- Optimism in situations where fear would be more appropriate
- Too great a belief in his own abilities
- Underrating the difficulties and complications of production and administration
- Taking on commitments with only a sketchy idea of how they will be met
- Dismissing, ignoring or not seeking cautious advice
- Seeing paperwork as dull (which it can be) and unnecessary (which it is not)
- Being inclined to lay out too much money on 'front' – fancy stationery, equipment, clothes, cars, premises and staff
- Being a 'sucker' for other salesmen's offerings
- Bullying colleagues who are trying to save him from his own folly.

These may be important weaknesses, but if they can be kept in check the good salesman's main worries will be about his tax bill. If he decides to operate as a partnership, the ideal partner will be someone who is good at administration and is not easily overcome by bullying. He should recognise that his lack of interest in paperwork and administration is a significant weakness and can cover for it in his selection of a partner or other associate. He should strenuously avoid other 'ideas' people; together they will build magnificent structures with the flimsiest foundations. Above all, he must pay attention to his colleagues' views, and allow them due weight. That they are spoken softly does not mean that they are valueless.

All this is important because, contrary to the views of some sales people, non-salesmen make an indispensable contribution to the health of a business. The accountant, the production manager, the distribution manager – all may look like pallid personalities to a flamboyant salesman. Nevertheless they make sure that his salary reaches him, they make the products that he sells, and they get them to the customers. Important though he is, the salesman is only one link in the chain, all the links being equally important. When he goes into business for himself the salesman still needs someone to fulfil these functions, and someone to exercise a restraining influence on his more ambitious excesses. Alone, he might be that figure beloved of romantic fiction, the glorious failure. With the right associates he can be a considerable success. The strengths that he brings to a business are the imagination to see new ways of doing things, the drive and determination to carry them out, and an ability to inspire his colleagues with his own energy and commitment. These strengths are enormously important and only too scarce in small businesses in Britain today.

The administrator

People who have spent a lifetime in administration usually exhibit all the sterling qualities of their calling. They are usually:

- Quiet
- Cautious
- Meticulous
- Ruthless in pursuit of precision
- Dedicated to exact observance of rules
- Inclined to seek rulings from above about deviations from the norm.

All businesses need access to these strengths, but they are not the qualities of which leaders are made. While the administrator is pursuing the missing 22p to make the books balance, someone else in the business may be making the firm £22,000 by exercising a very different set of skills. Not all administrators are good at their jobs, some having been forced into them by circumstances rather than choice. They may well survive in administration while not employing the more entrepreneurial skills that they might possess. The message for the administrator thinking of going into business for himself is to think hard before doing it. There is no shame in recognising that your talents lie elsewhere and in not going ahead, but the true administrator does not need to be told that: he is already doing it.

Let us take a more positive look at the administrator's potential in a small firm: many small firms have no formal systems to speak of, and although the owner may not realise it, may have a great need for the administrator's skills. It is important for the administrator not to apply a standard solution but to talk through with the entrepreneur what *he* thinks is needed and to arrive at an understanding of what truly makes the firm tick. Thus, he can help to ensure that the vital processes which really keep the firm going are not adversely affected by being brought under sound control. At the same time he should avoid installing controls which will not make any real difference to the firm's efficiency, effectiveness, or survival.

The administrator might not make much of a leader or be very good at selling, but he is an excellent Number Two to a visionary entrepreneur. Instead of setting out on his own, if the administrator lacks the imaginative drive to found a successful firm he could do a lot worse than hitch his wagon to the rising star of some wild man who has the gift of making things happen. Such people often have no grasp of proper systems, necessary administration, and their associated paperwork. The administrator's contribution to such a person's success could be a vital one, but it will not always be acknowledged. Indeed, he may get more kicks than thanks, but is it not characteristic that he takes satisfaction in being right, rather than in getting the limelight?

1.7 Your personal finances

A new businessman can feel like a financial untouchable. Until he has two or three years' successful trading behind him, financial people regard his income as insecure, and see him as a bit of a risk. This need not stand in his way when it comes to raising money for the firm (see section 4 on raising capital), but some personal matters should be cleared up first.

If you are in work and plan to buy a house, but have not yet done so, sign up for a mortgage while the building society can still get an employer's reference.

In planning for your business you will allow for some sort of income to yourself to cover living costs and household expenses. This will probably be some minimum figure so as not to put too great a strain on the firm. That makes sense, but it is also wise to make your plans show a rapid rise in your cash drawings from the firm to give you at least the full entitlement of an employee. When employed you are used to seeing deductions from gross pay to meet income tax, National Insurance and pension fund contributions, and perhaps other costs. But there are hidden subsidies to employees that you need to take into account when working out how much your business must earn to make good your lost income. For a start there is the employer's National Insurance contribution, about one tenth of your gross salary. Then there is the employer's pension contribution. That varies from scheme to scheme, but can be as high as one-quarter of your gross pay. Another tenth is accounted for by paid holidays and bank holidays. Use of a company vehicle is something you will certainly miss. Life insurance? Health insurance? And lunch allowances, and other perks? Somewhere there must be a saint who never misuses his employer's property, but the sinful photocopier as well. Some of those costs will be built into your financial plan, but others are personal perks that you will either have to do without or afford from the income the business pays you.

1.8 What sort of business to start?

If there is one clear rule, it is that there are few clear rules. Small business success stories include people who have stuck to a field that they know, as well as those who have broken into something quite new. Obviously, if you do not know much about a particular line of business it pays to find out as much as you can. It is surprising how often what is 'obvious' to the insider can be almost invisible to the newcomer. The Army has a wise saying – time spent on reconnaissance is seldom wasted. Whatever you do, avoid the get-rich-quick scheme that requires you to sign up straight away. Take time to map out the territory before leaping in. All this may sound elementary, but too many people repent at leisure decisions taken too hastily. I once met a couple who bought a hotel, sinking their life savings and taking a hefty loan. Only when they were installed did they realise that it was an eighteen-hour-day, seven-day-week business. The tragedy was that they had gone into it to give the wife the quiet life that her health needed.

This is not to say that no opportunity to make a good profit is ever genuine. The message is that probing and searching enquiry is essential in any circumstances, but specially so when you do not know the industry. One of the biggest enemies you will encounter is the natural human tendency to assume that things will work out well, just because that would be convenient.

A further influence on your choice might be the amount of money you can raise or are prepared to risk. If you want to minimise your investment you could look at a business that offers a service, rather than one that makes things, one that settles in cash as soon as the job is done, or even takes a deposit with the order, and does not need special premises. If you must make things it could be worth investigating having them made by a subcontractor at first. That might mean paying a higher price than you would wish, but it will have at least two powerful advantages: most of your time will be free for the vital job of selling, and you will not have to tie yourself down with premises right away. If things go well there will be plenty of time to set up your own workshop – if you find you really need one after all. Or you could set up a service operation concerned with your main line, get to know the users and build a reputation, and later go into the high-capital business of actually making the main line.

If your experience is in manufacturing, do not automatically assume that your business has to make things. Many successful service firms have been founded by people with production experience. For example, there is the engineer who, instead of making cutters for machine tools, identified a need for a quick-response tool-sharpening service. There is no limit to the number of possible approaches, and a little thought and imagination could get you into business realistically, leaving the big build-up for later when you have a track record to satisfy yourself and the bank. Even if your idea seems outlandish at first, remember that sometimes the standard formula wins, sometimes the completely new approach. There are few clear rules.

1.9 Taking up a franchise

Faced by the bewildering range of options open to him, the aspiring businessman might think that taking up a franchise could be the answer to his prayers. If he begins to make enquiries, he will quickly be on the receiving end of a parade of success stories and very persuasive sales techniques. No doubt the success stories can be proved to be true, but they might not reveal all that he needs to know. The first thing he must remember is that the person selling the franchise might stand to make much more out of the deal than he could ever earn from it.

We shall go into the main matters to be considered in a moment. First, a brief summary of how the system works.

If I have had a bright idea for a business, and for whatever reason I lack the desire or the resources to exploit it nationwide, I might think of franchising as a way of making some money from it. Let us suppose that I have proved that it works in a couple of establishments of my own. I can therefore show detailed costings, prices and profit margins, as well as the site layout (we shall assume, for this example, that it is a shop-based operation) and design that my experiments have developed. I decide to offer it as a franchise. I shall expect people to pay me a lump sum at the outset, and a royalty, probably based on their sales, each year. I might also insist that they buy some or all of their supplies from me, on which I shall take a cut.

You see my advertising, and pay me a visit. I shall probably hold a seminar in a plush hotel, with much razzmatazz and hard selling. You will come away with hope in your heart, hope that the dream I have described, of large sums of easy money, will come true. You are not stupid, but you are now in that most dangerous state of mind – you *want* to be sold! You are uncertain, and I am offering certainty. For your own good you must break the spell. Otherwise, you might just sign the agreement and hand over a cheque. Put your trust not in the yarn that I have spun, but in your own judgement, that part of you that says,

'There must be a catch in this somewhere.' Your uncertainty is correct; my certainty could well be an act designed to part you from your money as easily as possible within the law.

Franchising is a method employed by some highly respectable companies, who would not dream of behaving disreputably. At the same time, there is nothing to stop me from making the insubstantial offering in the convincing way that I have portrayed. If you go in for a franchise, you would do well to ask many searching questions of my imaginary operation and trust nothing I say that I cannot prove.

What can you expect from a reputable franchisor in return for your money? The main benefits are:

- Reduction in risk: tried and tested idea
- Advertising and public relations support
- Predetermined marketing, production and administration package, clearly defined in writing
- Package of finance
- Continuing support and help with problems.

Not all of these elements are present in all franchise offerings, but the general idea is always the same: somewhere there is a Mr Big who operates at the national level, while you run your own firm locally, which also happens to be his local branch. The best try to run the show in the spirit of partnership that will build a long-term relationship with franchisees, the worst more or less take your money and run.

Some key questions to ask yourself include:

- Does this particular franchise need experience of the trade, or could anyone with enough drive run it?
- Am I the right type of person for this business?
- What sort of franchise would suit my circumstances – one demanding equipment and premises, or one I could run all by myself, or what?
- Do they want a high initial fee, and a low royalty? Is this suspect?
- Can I finance it? (Costs range from £10,000 or less to over £¼m to set up.)
- Have I evaluated this proposition as carefully as I would my own business idea?

The advisory agencies can offer advice, and some banks employ franchising specialists. The British Franchise Association can give information (their address is in Section 15). You also ought to read a good book on the subject: one is *Taking up a Franchise* by Colin Barrow and Godfrey Golzen, published by Kogan Page. As always, care is called for in assembling and judging facts, and imagination needs to be balanced by scepticism. Needless to say, you should get advice from a good commercial solicitor. With any luck, the outcome will be a wise decision.

Marketing, Selling and Advertising

2.1 Aims of this section

'Marketing' aims to find out what the customer wants, and to supply it at a profit. It is the opposite of making whatever you like and then looking for someone to buy it. Good marketing aims to make it easy to get profitable sales, bad marketing may make it impossible. Good marketing can make profits from ordinary products, where poor marketing would cause losses. Without good marketing and effective selling your business will be like a car with no fuel and no driver. It can do only two things: sit there and rust, or run downhill. This section aims to equip you with the basic techniques for getting your business to go somewhere.

2.2 What are you selling?

At first glance this may seem a silly question. You know what you want to sell: let us say it is children's clothes. But that's not the whole answer; it does not fully describe what the customer really wants. The customer may want warmth and weather-proofing, or lightness, or fashion, or value for money, or good wear and long life, or good service (such as a no-quibble replacement guarantee), or twice-weekly delivery, or something else besides. The point is that you need to *know* – not just assume – what your customer really wants to buy, and then sell it to him. Often it is a combination of factors. You need to decide which are important and which are not.

2.3 Who will buy it?

The obvious answer is 'Customers, if anyone'. But who is the customer? A jobbing builder might say that the householder is his customer, a toymaker could say that mothers are, an engineer might cite engineering buyers. Certainly all of them are important, but so are the architect advising that householder, the child who doesn't like the colour, the engineering manager who trusts only his old friends at Smith & Jones. In each buying decision more than one person will have some sort of say, and every time the influence of these often unseen people will vary. One of your tasks is to understand how this works generally throughout your market and, in time, to know what the exact balance is for each of your customers. Obviously, you need to make sure that the people who really influence the decision have heard of you and approve of your proposition, even if they're not the ones you normally meet when you visit the customer.

2.4 How to find customers

Big companies' markets are made up of huge numbers of people. It is a real headache for them to find effective and efficient ways of telling their customers about the product. On the other hand, depending on the market it is in, a small firm usually finds the job of locating its customers much easier. The first step is to define the 'consumers' of your product, the people who will actually use it. Sometimes they place the order, sometimes someone else (a shop, perhaps) buys from you to provide it to the consumer. The consumer is the king in your business, and you place his or her interests slightly higher than your own. If you look after the consumer you should be able to make a living, but if you don't you are risking a lot.

Suppose your product sells to consumers through the shops. Suppose you supply something that the customer wants, yet the shops resist it. Do you give up, and bow down to the shop-keeper? You could, and in the short term you might be right. But sooner or later the consumer's need that you identified will be satisfied; as you thought of it first, why not by you? The example that springs to mind is of Tuf shoes inventing the six-month guarantee. Many shops hated it because of the effect on their repair trade, some disliked the administration involved, but Tuf kept on and became the biggest brand of men's shoes in the UK, and were paid the compliment of having their guarantee copied by most of their competitors. Of course, they had a war-chest which allowed them to go over the retailer's head direct to the consumer by way of TV advertising. Nonetheless, the example proves the point that it can pay off to put consumers higher than the dealers you have to use. But more often than not dealers will recognise it if you offer a better deal for their customers – your consumers.

To deal effectively with consumers you need to group them together: it would be difficult to reach people who have practically nothing in common, and probably impossible to design something that they all liked. Consumers of your product can be grouped together in all sorts of ways. For instance, on the basis of where they are geographically, or whether they use a lot of your product or a little, or by income group, or social class, or age, or leisure interests, or in many other ways. Once you have an identifiable group or groups you have a crystal-clear target for your whole marketing effort. If your consumers seem to fit into more than one overlapping grouping, so much the better. It defines the target more clearly. For instance, if you plan to service small motor-mowers, your main target could be owner-occupiers (not tenants) in housing with between 500 and 5000 square feet of lawn (those with less than 500 sq ft probably use hand-mowers; those with more than 5000 sq ft probably use a ride-on type), in the small towns or suburbs (small villages – too costly to reach; town centre – too few lawns), within a 10-mile radius (you aim to dominate your home area and will concentrate here). All these definitions are imaginary. In practice they would come from information on people's lawn-mowing habits gained from many sources.

Once you have decided on your target group(s) you can decide how to reach them, whether by direct selling or through other channels. The eventual aim is to select a group or groups with the biggest profit-potential, and which fits best with your resources. Before that final selection is made you need much more information on your market.

2.5 Information sources

It is surprising how much information on your market is available if only you know where to go for it. Much of it is in obvious places like Yellow Pages. Most large public libraries carry the Yellow Pages directories for the whole of the UK. Public libraries often have special commercial and technical sections, carrying a wide range of directories of all sorts as well as information on the bigger public companies and much else besides. Librarians can be incredibly helpful. They are trained for years in how to find out facts – indeed, some people call them information scientists – and can then be put in charge of collecting fines for overdue novels. Those that get into the library's commercial section are in their element and thoroughly enjoy helping you find what you want.

Other people with knowledge useful to you include local authorities (whose estates departments have lists of tenants of their industrial properties); local industrial promotion units, Chambers of Commerce, trade associations, business clubs (who have lists of businesses), colleges, your bank and your accountant, who have knowledge and contacts. But probably one of your best information sources is your own knowledge of your industry, coupled with your own eyes and ears. If you are selling home extensions you will probably look for areas housing young, growing families – the modern, owner-occupied, housing estates which you can see with your own eyes.

The more specialised your target groups of customers are, the more likely they are to be served by magazines, clubs, and so forth. This goes for anglers, training officers, and plumbers, just as much as for the professions and farmers and any other groups you can think of. Their clubs and institutes usually publish membership lists which anyone can consult. The smaller ones have noticeboards and newsletters and the larger ones will be served by magazines: both will give you valuable information on developments among your customers and give you sales leads galore. Some trade magazines run surveys among readers and may sell you old issues that contain survey reports. Most market research surveys are privately commissioned and are not supplied to all comers. Some exceptions include the more lively trade bodies and associations – tourist boards and training boards, for example, carry out a lot of research and make it available.

Possibly the best sources of really good reports on different markets are EIU (Economist Intelligence Unit) and Mintel. Every month they each publish a magazine containing a number of well-researched articles on different markets. While it is costly to subscribe direct, many larger public libraries and college libraries do keep them. The 20-odd overseas department stores who buy through the London-based EXBO might be interested in you. Finally, the Department of Trade and Industry publishes a lot of statistics which are kept by large libraries.

2.6 Forecasting your sales

This is a vitally important activity. It is also difficult to get right, even when you have plenty of experience in your business, and is therefore a big problem for the new starter. From the sales forecast flow most of the big decisions in the business. It governs how many people you need to employ, what equipment, what size of premises, how much cash. In turn, if any of these is already fixed, it is a limitation on the sales forecast: you would be crazy to sell more than you could make on your equipment, for instance. (No sensible businessman would take that statement at face value, of course. If he saw the chance of making more profit than his machines would let him, he would try to find a way round the problem. Two examples that spring to mind are upgrading the equipment or contracting out some of the production, but only if it can be done profitably.) Also, the sales forecast sets standards to compare with actual results.

Before any comparison can take place, however, a forecast must first be made. Wishful thinking, 'something will turn up' – forget it. No one owes you a living. No one will give you an order unless you have a proposition that they like and which you have put across clearly. You will have designed your proposition by now and tested it out on a few people in the target market, no doubt, and feel finally that you are getting it right. Now is the time to test it out in earnest. Why not visit potential customers to see what they say? Stress that it is only a research visit, and encourage them to speak critically as well as in praise. It is not a selling call, you are there to learn from them, and since you are not paying for their valuable time the least you can do is listen. Construct a simple questionnaire to remind you to ask all the questions, and get at least 30 replies from people who are truly in the target market. Thirty, the statisticians tell us, is the smallest number that can safely be taken as a sample representing everyone in a group. One problem of person-to-person market research is that most people don't like to hurt the interviewer's feelings and will often give a kind answer rather than a truthful one. Others will pooh-pooh your proposition through nastiness or in the hope of driving the price down. Equally, on a research visit you cannot present your proposition as energetically and persistently as on a 'live' call – would you have swayed more people if you had actually been selling? There can be no general answer, so you need to keep your wits about you to assess what people really mean and how they will probably behave, and adjust your forecast accordingly.

Because it is fraught with such uncertainty, the best method for many people is to start the business off on a small scale, perhaps part time, perhaps with someone else making the product initially. Once you have gained some experience it will be easier to forecast sales and you will have greater confidence that the whole operation will work. Some people feel this is so important that they don't mind making no profit, or even a small loss, on this 'test-bench' approach. One vital piece of financial planning can be done at this stage: a check can be made that you can reasonably expect to achieve at least the minimum level of sales to cover the firm's likely costs. (See also section 3.)

2.7 The proposition you are selling

Customers don't buy products, they buy propositions. That is to say, there is much more to the offer you make your customer than just a product at the lowest price. Take an example that everyone recognises, of someone buying a shirt from Marks & Spencer: M & S are hugely successful, yet their prices are comparatively high – twice as much as the local market traders charge. They can get those high prices because they offer much more than a shirt: there is the convenience of high street shopping, easy self-selection, acceptable styling, good standards of quality backed by a guarantee, no-quibble exchange (or even a refund), helpful assistants, acceptance of cheques, and a pleasant, clean environment. Marks & Spencer take much more money from the customer than it costs to provide these extras, as their extraordinary profits show. What is more, the customers love it. None of that just happened, it is the result of a century of painstaking observation of customers' behaviour and research into their needs, and rigorous analysis of competitors' offerings coupled with a powerful determination to increase profits all the time.

M & S have been built up on one successful formula, but it is not the only one available. There are many smaller firms selling shirts more individually styled at even higher prices from suburban locations (easy parking) or city centre sites (near concentrations of rich customers). So there is no single formula for success, but an attitude of mind that fixes on what the consumer really needs (which isn't always what he says he wants), and provides it at a profit. And that is where this whole section started.

2.8 What the customer says he wants

There can be a big gap between what customers say they want and what they actually buy. This may be partly because what they want is not available, and partly due to salesmanship. But the main reason is that what they say they want, and what they really need, can be very different indeed. An engineer might be anxious to cut his bill for small tools – twist drills and the like. He will say he wants to buy cheaper. If you take that literally and import lots of cheap drill-bits you could look very sick, even if they are only one-tenth of the price of the domestic product, because few engineers would trust their performance. What the customer *really* needed was a lower price for the same quality, or better quality pieces perhaps at a higher price still. Or he might just need a better system for controlling his stores so that fewer go missing – always assuming, that is, that he is getting what he is paying for, and that the high costs are not due to some fiddle involving fake bills for deliveries that were never made. Only detailed understanding of how your chosen market works will enable you to see the difference between your customer's wants and needs.

2.9 What the customer really needs

In the last example above, the customer's real need might have been an overhaul to his accounting system. If instead he had bought some low-quality tools from you he would probably accuse you of selling rubbish, even though the low price should have warned him. So one lesson to be learned is that the price alone is not as important as people make it out to be. What *is* important is the price *for a given level of quality:* another word for it is 'value'. Following Marks & Spencer's lead, you will try to make your proposition more valuable than a competitor's, and to do it for less than the extra that the customer will pay for it.

To see how to add value to your proposition you must know what customers really need. Look at every part of the propositions currently on offer. Do competitors deliver monthly? If you deliver weekly or fortnightly customers need to carry less stock and can get urgent 'specials' more quickly. Do competitors deliver weekly? Perhaps you could deliver twice a week? Or monthly, making bigger deliveries and charging lower prices as a result. Most of the time customers will assume that the service they get now is all that could ever be on offer. It needs you to ask them the deeper questions to open up what they really need. Until you ask if a more frequent delivery would help their whole business it won't occur to them that it is possible. That, in turn, makes it important to speak to all the right people. The production foreman can't be blamed for preferring the existing arrangements, and for not seeing any advantage in more frequent delivery. The works manager, who has to perform the balancing act between having enough stock but not too much, should see the point straight away. This whole approach applies to the entire proposition on offer, not just to frequency of delivery: look at everything from the customer's point of view and help him to perform better. He will pay you to. And he will rarely pay you for offering the same or less than your competitors, so you need to know them well too.

2.10 Why customers should buy from you, not from your competitor

Apart from monopolies, shortages and blood-ties, customers will buy only because you have constructed a more relevant proposition (that's marketing) and put it across well (selling). There is no other basis for building a business legally. Without that basis there is no point in spending time wondering about finance, equipment, premises, or any other matter. Once the business is launched you do not stop thinking about why customers should buy from you, for you in turn become the target for some energetic, bright youngster who is just starting up. To defend yourself from him, and to keep yourself ahead of the established firms you are attacking, you must keep this question under constant review, and continually strengthen the reasons for your customers to come to you.

Before starting up, ask yourself: what will you look like to a customer? Fairly normal, you might say. But you need to look like rather more than that. A lot of hot air is talked about 'image', but there is sound business common sense behind it. See it from the customer's point of view: all he knows about your firm is probably sight of a letter, a brochure, a vehicle and a person (you). He is interested in profitable propositions, but also busy, maybe harassed. He will make up his mind in a few seconds whether or not to take your proposal further. The risks of being 'dustbinned' are so much less if everything about the firm looks attractive. To achieve that, it is worth using a professional designer. He or she will:

- Look at your firm from its customer's point of view
- Express its proposition by means of graphic design
- Ensure a consistent look to all of your contacts with customers.

'All of your contacts with customers' means just that: letterheads, typewriter typeface, business cards, brochures, staff uniforms (yes, even a one-man firm can have a few T-shirts or overalls printed quite cheaply), vehicle livery, showroom appearance, and so on. Think, too, of whether or not you wear a suit (if so, should it be dark and formal, tweedy, or what?), or a white overall or dungarees, or whatever. Discuss this with the designer too. Do not think that this is fanciful, or that it need be expensive. Remember the speed with which the customer makes up his mind, and improve your chances by looking really good. As for the expense, it need not cost much and ought to pay for itself if you do it wisely. You will spend money on some of these things anyway, and by spending as little as £200 more you could get a lot better value.

Before selecting your designer, get him to talk about the kind of thing he can do for you. If there is the slightest suggestion that you buy really expensive writing paper, especially if it is coloured, be careful. He might not be thinking of *your* best interests – have you ever tried to buy typewriter-correcting fluid, or correcting paper, for tinted writing paper? Most of it is white, so if you must have tinted paper either do not make typing mistakes, or buy a typewriter with a correcting ribbon that automatically lifts the wrong letter off the page completely. As for the really expensive writing paper, the sort that needs a crowbar to unfold it, it costs the earth and can actually put people off by looking too opulent. So pick the designer who looks at the problem right through to how his solutions will be implemented and how you will use the materials. This goes right down to the level of choosing standard colours – white for letter-heads, as already suggested, and vehicle manufacturers' normal colours for vans and so forth – to keep down the cost of putting the designs into practice. If your designer does not look at the problem this way, he must have a really good reason or he is not a true designer. And, as with every supplier, get a written quote first and do not spend a penny more than you must.

2.11 Getting the product to the customer

Not a section on transport, but about whether you sell direct to the user or through middlemen. Shops, wholesalers, distributors, factors, stockists, agents, and so on, can do a useful job, but they might not suit your business. They also want a profit for themselves. On the other hand, selling direct to the customer on the doorstep, by direct mail, party plan, mail order, market stalls, or the telephone, does get you the full price but takes time and costs money. Equally, you might be able to do both, allocating the job of selling to different parts of your market to whoever does it best. To help you to decide, consider:

- If you give the selling job entirely to someone else, who will have the whip hand, you or the salesperson?
- Can anyone else be better than you at selling your product?
- Which makes more money for you, selling or making?
- If you decided to drop either selling or making, what would it cost to get someone to do what you drop, taking into account that he would not do it as well as you do?
- If the chips were down, who would survive – the salesman who refused to hand over the order, or the maker who refused to deliver the goods?
- If you don't do the selling, can you somehow keep up your knowledge of customers' changing needs, other than by relying on the seller to tell you?

Some businesses force you to deal direct with the customer – an emergency plumber who sent out a salesman to look at the job would seem a bit strange. That does not mean that the plumber could not have links with other emergency services who could put work his way, but that in his case the operative has also to be the salesman for each individual job. For most manufacturing and service firms, however, the choice of selling direct or through other channels does exist. The way not to make the choice is by personal preference. If you hate being cooped up all day, that does not make you the best salesman in your firm. If, on the other hand, you just don't like selling, you might still be better employed as an average salesman than as a disastrous production manager. You have to decide on the basis of what is best for your customers and for your firm, and then single-mindedly carry it out. Your business should give you pleasure and satisfaction but it will survive to do so only if you shoulder the full responsibility for running it. If that sometimes means doing unpleasant things yourself, so be it.

So far this section has assumed that a real opportunity exists to find a sales agent. ('Sales agent' means a freelance salesperson who sells and takes orders, no more, for a commission of usually between 10 and 15 per cent of the value of the sales he makes. You pay him when the customer pays you. Other frills can be added – perhaps he will agree to carry a small stock of your product in his vehicle for emergency restocking, or chase up slow payers, or undertake other services. He sells other people's products too.) Sales agents will only sell lines that are profitable to them, which means that either your product must sell easily and quickly, or you must offer an above-average commission. A written agreement needs to be made, laying down each side's duties and expectations. Good agents can be very difficult for the new small firm to find. The places to look are in the back of your trade press, or you can try the British Agents' Register, or the Manufacturers' Agents' Association (addresses in section 13). You could advertise for an agent in your trade press, or ask shops, and ask manufacturers of associated (but not competing) products to give you the name of theirs. Whatever you do, one is unlikely to come running to you in your early days, and the costs of finding one can be well into three figures.

2.12 Selling direct to the customer

This method does help you keep a finger on the pulse of what is going on. If your proposition is wrong you don't get orders; if you don't put it across clearly to the right people, the same applies. Simple, direct, brutal. You learn very quickly that something is wrong, but finding out just what it is takes longer. Dealing direct with customers gives you the chance to adjust the proposition, to try new emphases – but don't change more than one thing at a time, and do test each version out on more than a handful of prospective customers before rejecting it. When you sell direct you also have more profit margin to play with than if you were selling through an agent, which hopefully compensates for extra time taken. Even if you have a genuine choice, it can be best to sell direct in the early stages of your business. That way you learn more about your customers and you could have more control over your destiny. If you have never done any commercial selling before this advice can seem frightening. But you have no alternative – you need to know your customers' needs, you are the only person who will take the trouble to discern what they really are, and no one else will be more committed to your success. After all, if your product fails completely, 100 per cent of your business is down the drain. To a distributor it might be only 5 or even 0.5 per cent of his total sales – a flea-bite.

2.13 Dealing direct with the public

The most popular methods are:

- *Doorstep selling*, used by, among others, Avon Cosmetics, encyclopaedia publishers and double glazing firms.
- *Mail order*, either off-the-page selling, where the customer sends in an order on the strength of the advertisement, or sales from the catalogue or data sheet which the ad asks them to write in for (though not sales through the big mail order catalogues, which get the whole of section 2.33 to themselves); see also section 2.34.
- *Direct mail*, which uses letterbox leafleting, leaflets under windscreen wipers or sales letters to selected sales prospects – you don't have to deliver them yourself, but can use the local newsagent; or the Post Office will quote a few pence per leaflet for delivery – more in section 2.35.
- *Market stalls* at craft shows, public markets, agricultural shows and other events.
- *Street selling*, like the fish-and-chip van, ice-cream van, and vegetable van; some forms of street trading need a licence, so check with the police.
- *Party plan*, used by Tupperware and thousands of imitators.
- *Showroom selling* from your own premises.
- *Mobile showrooms*, often a converted trailer or family caravan.
- *Telephone selling*, used more in North America than here, but extremely useful for setting up appointments for demonstrations, and very cost-effective for getting top-up orders once the initial sale has been made (but it should not replace all personal sales contact) – see section 2.36.
- *Piggyback leaflets*, such as a seat-cover catalogue in every new car.

There are many more – just look around. More media still are being developed, as electronics push back communication frontiers. The great things are not to overlook an opportunity because you cannot immediately see an application in your field, and not to dismiss it because of prejudice. Instead, seek out ideas used in other industries and ask yourself how they could be put to work for you. That approach could make you the inventor of the next big breakthrough.

If you mean to sell through the shops at the same time as selling direct to the public, be careful. To start with, you should sell at the same price, or no less, than the shops. Otherwise they will be annoyed at your undercutting them. Some shopkeepers may be jealous even then, so it is worth thinking about using a different brand or trading name for dealings with shops from the one you use to the public. Some people even use a different address, too. Another method of avoiding the wrath of the shopkeeper is to run ads for the product which say '... Available from good (grocers? chemists?) everywhere, or in case of difficulty direct from the manufacturer at (address).'

2.14 The middleman's cut

Every middleman has to cover his costs and make a profit, like any other businessman. Moreover, as his supplier, you will want him to be profitable so that he stays in business and keeps on buying. Some people get heated about how much profit middlemen take, without understanding the costs they have to meet. That is pointless. It is a fact of life and must be accepted and allowed for. If a competitor can sell to a shop or a distributor and allow him his normal mark-up, but you find it impossible to do so, one of you is doing something very wrong. Needless to say, you have to be absolutely certain it is not you. *Absolutely* certain, for a mistake like that could be fatal. And before you depress yourself too much, be sure you are comparing like with like. Anyone can sell more cheaply if he uses the cheapest material and assembles it without real care. On the other hand, it is difficult to compete head-on with the prices charged by someone who has more and better machines than you. Better not pick the fight in the first place, but go instead for a gap which that competitor cannot satisfy.

2.15 How the shops calculate their selling prices

Whether you sell industrial goods through distributors or consumer goods through shops, you need to understand how they work out their prices. Most trades have their traditional profit margins based roughly on how fast goods in particular trades sell, and on what risks exist. They are all worked out in the same way. Take tinned beans: they don't go out of fashion, or go bad, and most families buy them at least once a month. Therefore the shops make very little on them – perhaps 10p in every £1. Some fresh fruit, on the other hand, needs more careful storage and handling, and often cannot be sold on Monday if it is left over on Saturday. Therefore the shop might keep 20p or 30p of every £1-worth sold. High-fashion clothing is an extreme example of risk: the stock can go out of fashion almost overnight, it is easily spoiled in storage, it needs high-rental premises in a good area, expensive decor and fittings, presentable staff, and it is easily stolen. It is therefore not unusual for at least half of the takings to go towards shop expenses and profit. In many trades the picture is confused by promotional offers, often inspired by manufacturers who temporarily reduce a price. It is further complicated by people using terms like 'mark-up', 'gross profit' and 'margin' or 'gross margin' as if they meant the same thing, which they do not. An example might help:

Cost to shop	£10.00	
Shop adds 50 per cent of its cost	£5.00	This is 'mark up' of 50 per cent on cost; 'margin' or 'gross margin' of 33⅓ per cent on selling price excluding VAT. It is also 'margin', 'gross margin', 'gross profit' or 'mark-up' of £5.
Shop's selling price excluding VAT	£15.00	Usually worked out separately as VAT doesn't give profit to the shop.
VAT at 15 per cent	£2.25	
Price to public	£17.25	The price-tag in the window

Even in this simple illustration there are as many as seven answers to the question, 'What profit do you make on this product?' To make sure that you understand what the answer really means, ask each trader you deal with exactly how he does his sums, using the example of something costing £1 or £10 – or £1000 or £10,000 if you are in that league. Of course, the canny shopkeeper who sees something that his customers will pay £17.45 for will not price it at £17.25. It may look like only a few pence to you, but if he sells 100 of them a year the difference in his profit is £20, enough to pay the young assistant's wages for a day. So the canny manufacturer – you – takes the price to the public of £17.45 and works back to a price to charge the shop. Taking that same product, now selling to the public at £17.45, our arithmetic looks like this:

Cost to shop	£10.11	(e)
Shop adds 50 per cent of its cost	£5.06	(d)
Shop's selling price excluding VAT	£15.17	(c)
VAT at 15 per cent	£2.28	(b)
Price to public	£17.45	(a)

Once you know the way the retailer calculates his prices, you can work out what he paid for anything in the shop. Using the example above, this is how you do it:

$c = a \div 1.15$ (or divide by 1.16 if VAT is at 16 per cent and so on)

$b = a - c$

$\quad = c \times 0.15$ (or multiply by 0.16 if VAT is at 16 per cent and so on)

$d = c \times \dfrac{50}{150}$ (or $c \times \dfrac{m}{100 + m}$, where m = the percentage

mark-up on cost price)

$e = c - d$

If any of this seems puzzling, get a bright 14-year-old with a calculator to take you through it. Youngsters handle figures all the time, and are trained to tackle questions like this. It is worth persevering with, for once you understand the formula you can almost instantly know what your competitors are charging your potential customers. If the 14-year-old has a computer, he or she will probably be able to write a simple program to make the calculation for you.

2.16 Which shops to sell to

Having a clear picture of the people who will buy your product, you will know the sort of shops they use. In your own town you know where to find those shops, but how do you find them in strange towns? The answer lies in asking the shops you do know about their counterparts, watching for ads in local papers, contacting Chambers of Trade (often separate from Chambers of Commerce), checking through Yellow Pages and trade directories, asking trade associations, and plain footslogging.

2.17 Why should shopkeepers bother to talk to you?

Not all will. Some - a few - may even be downright rude. But the intelligent ones will see you, as well as the ones who cannot get credit or supplies elsewhere (for this latter category see section 3.17 on minimising credit risks). As a businessman you will aim to get all successful retailers as your customers, not just the polite ones, so a thick skin and broad back are essential (see sections 2.22 to 2.29 on selling and salesmanship). The shopkeeper approached by a new supplier knows from experience that only one salesman in a hundred really has what he wants. He also knows that you may be that person. It is part of the selling task to fan that tiny glow of curiosity to the point where, however gracelessly, the shopkeeper agrees to see you. Moreover, the shopkeeper in your own town who refuses to see you risks losing you and your friends as customers, so he will probably be polite. Finally, the preparation you have done and the planned way in which you make your case, having good answers ready, will earn respect for your business and the way that you manage it.

One key item of your planning will be to avoid visiting shops to sell things when they are busy (market days, weekends, lunch-times) and, of course, on early closing days. Early closing and market day information is in public library gazetteers and in motoring organisations' handbooks.

2.18 What the shopkeeper is looking for

If you know what he wants you have a better idea of how to sell to the shopkeeper, or for that matter to anyone. In an ideal world he would have goods that were:

- Demanded by his customers without prompting
- Exclusive to him, at least in his area
- Not affected by season or fashion
- Unlikely to spoil in storage
- Difficult to steal
- Compact and easy to handle
- Faultlessly reliable
- Cheaper than competitive goods.

He would also like the company supplying them to:

- Keep plenty of stock of all varieties, colours, sizes etc
- Have an instant delivery system
- Offer high profit margins
- Give plenty of support by way of free display material, display stands, heavy advertising that mentions his name, contribution to his own advertising costs, and incentive bonuses that require little effort to win
- Offer unlimited credit
- Be entirely dependable and honest in all its dealings
- ... And a lot more besides.

Obviously, there are contradictions in all this, so remember that it describes a shopkeeper's ideal world. In the real world it is simply not realistic to expect, for instance, a product that is both heavily advertised and restricted to only one outlet, or for a fresh food product to have indefinite shelf-life. Retailers realise this. So what do they *really* expect, and what should you offer?

2.19 What you can offer

To get two problem areas out of the way first: it is rare that a small firm can make as good a product and offer as good a service more cheaply than other firms. Many would contest that statement, but the small firm that cuts prices is usually cutting something else to pay for it. Even when someone does break the rule successfully he could then find that two things happen: he is swamped with orders and annoys customers by keeping them waiting, and then his competitor responds with a bigger price cut. That shortens his waiting list, but if he has to hit back it cuts his profits too.

Offering higher margins to the trade can be a useful ploy short term, but is fraught with danger long term. In effect it is the same as price cutting, something to be undertaken only after the most serious consideration. All things considered, the shopkeeper wants you to offer goods that will keep his customers happy. To do that they must offer better value than competitive goods. For himself he will look for good service and normal margins. Follow these principles and you should not go far wrong. At the same time, look out for low-cost ways of offering distinctly better service in a relevant manner.

A key point to remember is that few shop assistants ever sell anything. Most let customers browse and buy, confining their own activity to collecting the money and topping up the shelves. Thus anything sold through shops has to be packaged and presented attractively: if the pack does not sell it, nothing else will. Needless to say, the packaging should be relevant to the product and to the way that the consumer sees the product. If the product is fragile it needs packaging that protects; if its main appeal is as a gift it should look like one, and so on.

Display material may be needed to draw attention to the product and invite purchase. This is a specialised area, so get advice from a design or advertising agency with experience in this field. The material can range from a simple pack-crowner (a showcard that fits on top of the pack) to a full-blown display rack costing hundreds of pounds. Remember that if the product is to sell out of the shop it must be easy for the shop's customers to buy. For that to happen they need to see it and understand what it is for. Get a few shopkeepers and a marketing specialist from one of the advisory agencies to comment before you commit yourself finally: they could save you from an expensive mistake. And if you do supply that expensive display stand, make sure that your customer understands that it is only on loan, and signs for it on that basis, and that it is clearly and indelibly marked to that effect. If he uses it to display competitors' products, or goes broke and disappears, you then have a chance of getting it back.

2.20 Sale or return

You may be asked to deliver goods on 'sale or return' (SOR). This means that the shop pays for them only if it sells them, and if it doesn't you can have them back. In some trades this is the done thing – some art galleries, for instance, offer display facilities and little else. But for the vast majority of trades it means one of two things: either the shopkeeper is not convinced enough by your proposition (in which case your sales technique or the proposition itself isn't right, or he isn't in your target market), or he has no money (in which case you should avoid him).

People can be tempted to accept SOR, particularly when times are hard, but they often find that when they go back to the shop after a month or two the goods aren't there, and there is a dispute about whether they were delivered at all, or about the terms of the agreement, or an outright refusal to pay. If the goods are actually there to be taken back they have often been poorly displayed and have become damaged or soiled, and thus of little use to the supplier. All in all, it is a pretty bad arrangement. The retailer gets a margin partly to cover the costs of carrying stock, and partly to compensate for taking risks with his buying, so why should he get the *whole* margin for doing only *part* of his job? And if he has paid for some of his stock items and not for others, which will he try harder to sell? If you are asked for SOR, decline gracefully and change the subject back to the benefits to him of stocking your product.

2.21 Selling to wholesalers and stockists

Much of what has been said about shops applies to these categories, but there is an important extra dimension – their sales forces. There are also sales people in shops, but either the shop is small or it is divided into small sections. Thus the relevant sales staff in a shop have a good chance to see your products when they are unpacked and displayed (although it is no bad idea to get the manager's approval for you to check with the staff that they do know what is special about your goods: few will bother to find out for themselves). In contrast, a wholesaler's salesman rarely gets more than a fleeting glance at your new product among all the others, and thereafter sees it by chance, if at all, on his customers' shelves. It is therefore vital to get to the salesmen, preferably by a personal presentation to their sales meeting. Ideally, this would be backed up by an incentive scheme (see sales promotion, section 2.32). If the customer won't let you see the salesman, at least get the incentive scheme in. That way you have a fighting chance of being seen among the 4000 or more lines which many wholesale salesmen deal with.

2.22 Preparing to call on a customer

You will have done some research, however basic (like looking in his window), to see if he is your kind of customer. You may have asked around, and even have taken out a credit reference report on him. You could have sought out and studied his advertising, which tells you a lot about him and his attitudes. You will be prepared for any eventuality once you get inside the door. But before you even set off on your first day's selling there are certain items you will need. They include:

- Price-lists
- Terms and conditions of sale (see section 6.12)
- Order form (or enquiry form if yours is the sort of product that is specially made and quoted for)
- Calculator
- Pencils (two, sharpened – a single one *always* breaks)
- Pens (two)
- Note pad
- Visiting cards
- Diary
- Worked illustrations of selling prices, savings, incentive bonuses etc
- Photographs
- Samples – Comparisons with competitors' performance
  - Advertising plans and layouts
  - Press cuttings
  - Display material
- A smart case to carry it all in.

All this should be clean and neatly arranged. One good thing to buy is a loose-leaf ring-binder-cum-clipboard. In the ring binder you can put clear plastic sleeves in which to keep your documents and photographs in the right order, and the clipboard holds order forms and a note pad. They usually have pockets for spare price-lists, customer record cards and so on. The importance of neatness and cleanliness cannot be over-emphasised. Your customer sees you infrequently and briefly, so do make a good impression every time. If you look scruffy or ill organised your customer cannot be blamed for thinking that you are a little like that all the time, and place his business elsewhere.

2.23 On entering the customer's premises

This is his territory on which you are an uninvited guest, so behave accordingly. You need not grovel, but should behave with dignity and, above all, courtesy. If the buyer, or the person who looks like the buyer, is already talking to a salesman, don't hang around but leave immediately. Come back later when the coast is clear. If there is a receptionist or assistant, introduce yourself and ask if you may see the buyer. Ask for his name and initials (and check spelling), and write them down. Even if the answer is disappointing, treat him or her and everyone else you meet with unfailing pleasantness (can *you* recognise a managing director's daughter or second cousin at a glance?). Play safe, be nice to everyone. You may even find you develop a relationship with receptionists whereby they want to help and actually give you hints on how to get to see the boss, but it will happen only if you're nice to them. Avoid over-familiarity.

Give the person who greets you your card, to save them from having to remember your name. If it is not the person you need to see, you might write a note on the back of your card such as: 'Mr Johnson'; (you *are* sure he spells it Johnson?). 'We should like to acquire a local stockist for our profitable new product. Could you spare five minutes, please, to talk about it? Peter Jones.' Or: 'Mrs Edwards: a small, low-cost swarf compactor for small machine shops. May I have an appointment to demonstrate (5 minutes), please. John James.' Or: 'Mr Harrison: new, locally-made, exclusive, fashion knitwear. Please can we discuss? Anthony Smith.' And so on. If you find yourself in a waiting room with other salesmen, quiz them discreetly about the customer – does he pay? What ploys does he use to unsettle salesmen? What are his biggest-selling lines? Ask about everything you need to know. Ask about other local firms too. Many salesmen like to show off their knowledge and to help a newcomer – cash in when you get the chance, and get to know better your customer's needs, methods, plans and weaknesses.

2.24 With the buyer

Respect your customer, his intelligence, and his time. At the same time, recognise that he will not know your product and proposition as well as you do, and to save time he will be tempted to assume that yours are just like the others. Create opportunities to contrast your product with those of competitors. Don't attack or criticise them destructively, especially if the customer uses them at present – to do that would be to attack his decision to stock those items. How to strike the balance? Not, 'Of course, Smith's stuff is rubbish. We wouldn't dream of making cheap garbage like that. It beats me how any engineer in his right mind could run the risk of using it,' but rather, 'We take a different view from your other suppliers. They aim their product mainly at the mass market, and we respect that decision, but we try to tailor ours for the special needs of the small precision engineer like you. Mr James, would I be right in thinking that your whole company stands or falls by the quality of its output?' (Pause – wait for the answer – he can hardly say 'No'.) 'Special products like ours do give you the absolutely vital reassurance that your quality will be maintained and, for that huge gain, they cost very little more. Let me show you how it works ...' Get him to talk about his needs and problems, ask questions and listen, really listen, to the answers. Don't let pass a single chance of showing how your product does meet his needs. Don't fight over his objections, but welcome them – he is taking you seriously and thinking about your proposition – but turn them to your advantage. Don't overstay your welcome.

Even if you are a first-rate comic, don't tell jokes until you know the buyer really well, if then. The trouble with jokes is that many of them rely on making someone look silly and are therefore offensive to that someone. Your hilarious story about Irishmen/Pakistanis/a sexual encounter/a disabled person could offend someone with Irish in-laws or with a Pakistani wife, a prude, or someone with a handicapped child. So why take the risk of telling such a story to someone whose background you don't know? Forget the idea that you must have a fund of jokes to stand a chance of selling anything. Moreover, jokes take up your customer's valuable time.

Try to avoid giving offence by using first names prematurely. And when you need to know it, do not ask for his Christian name, but for his first name or forename – not everyone is a Christian.

2.25 Planning your sales presentation

To some extent every presentation to a customer needs planning individually. In different trades the method of presentation may vary, but there are certain basic rules which apply everywhere all the time. To start with, there is the basic framework of your approach, summarised by the word AIDA, the initial letters of:

Attention
Interest
Desire
Action.

Your first task is to get the buyer's *attention*. That's easy – he's looking at you, isn't he? But is he concentrating on your story, or still thinking about the chance he missed to make a killing with a special offer this morning, or how soon he can get rid of you to chase up Tomlinson's last order, or how he's going to deal with that awkward memo from the MD, or whether his wife will still be in a bad mood when he gets home? If you fail to focus his attention on your proposition, he will hardly notice that you've been there.

Once you have got his attention, you need to get him *interested* and involved in what you are offering, so that he moves towards the next stage, *desire* for your product. When that's arrived at, the order isn't guaranteed: you have to get *action*, that agreement to place an order.

Analyse those gems of selling, good TV commercials. See how they tackle the selling job in the same way, while sticking to a few main points and putting them across clearly. Practise your story and try to perfect ways of getting your points over vividly.

2.26 Getting attention

Obviously you can get attention by extraordinary behaviour, but the whole tone of your presentation must match the tone of your proposition. The best way of getting attention will vary from buyer to buyer, and from call to call on the same buyer. A general-purpose approach for someone who is not used to selling might be to boil down the whole proposition to a few questions. The questions should be phrased so as to leave no possibility of disagreement. Example: 'Am I right in thinking you would like to cut down stocks if you dared?' ('Of course.') 'That if you could, you would have fewer space problems, less stock-control trouble, and fewer stock losses?' ('Naturally.') 'I would like to take a little of your time to show you how we can help you do just that, while maintaining – indeed improving – your service to customers.' (The proposition is that you offer faster delivery and better stocks, so that customers don't have to carry so much stock themselves.) The customer is really listening now, as you've hit on an area of interest to all businesses. But he needs to know how you are going to perform this miracle before he can believe in it, so he is eager to hear more, though still sceptical.

2.27 Getting interest

When he is interested, the buyer will be comparing your proposition with his experience and his needs. That will give him both favourable and unfavourable feelings towards you. You're new, so you will make an effort to give service, but you're also untried and may turn out to be unreliable. Your product will cut costs, probably, but will need capital outlay for certain. And so on. By now, you are telling your story of how the product works, and why, and pointing out the advantages to him. Get him to react to each point: 'Is that right?', 'What happens in your experience, Mr Adams?' Many of the questions you ask in this phase are open-ended, for if he thinks there is a basic flaw in your proposition you want that flushed out as soon as it arises. You can then deal with it, but not if you press on regardless. Watch out for bodily restlessness. It probably means he disagrees, or is dying to say something but can't get a word in, or wants to get rid of you as fast as possible. If you notice it, stop and ask a question. Try to prevent it from happening in the first place by stopping at natural breaks and checking that he has understood, is still concentrating and still interested – again, a question does the trick. The phrasing of questions matters. Not, 'Have you understood me so far?' (ie, you do look a bit thick), but rather, 'I hope I've managed to make myself clear?' (ie, although I do my best, my explanations are possibly not as good as your obviously razor-sharp mind deserves). Now that you have established real interest in the proposition, you need to move him on to wanting it for himself.

2.28 Desire for the product

The dividing line between each of these sections is sometimes clear, sometimes blurred. But we all recognise a distinction in our own minds between merely liking the idea of a product and actually wanting one ourselves. There are many products that we like and admire and can afford, but that we do not actually want. So it is vital to move your buyer from mere interest to real desire for the product. What is the bridge across that gap? Often it is the buyer's mind making the leap to imagining what it would be like to own the product, and how much better his life would be if he did. Most buyers need help in making that leap, in visualising the benefits. Keep and develop his interest and desire by personalising the points you have made and agreed on. 'Now let's look at what it would do for your business, Mr Elton. We've agreed you would save £2 a unit. How many a day do you make?' ('25, sometimes more.') 'So what's that you'd save every day? £2 times 25 – what's that per week?' ('Er, £50 a day, £250 a week.') '£250 a week: £12,000 a year – could you find a use for that?' Could he just! Once that idea has been planted and taken root you are ready to take things to the next stage, of acting on his desire.

2.29 Action: getting the order

This is the most agonising part of the discussion for both of you. Your anxiety is easy to understand, and so is his. Up to now everything has been on a fairly theoretical level, an interesting conversation about possibilities. Now you have spoilt it all by asking for an order. Of course, he expected it because he knows you have a living to make. Human beings are able to kid themselves, though, so this is often the place where you really start to sell. Up to now he's been agreeing with you, you've got along famously, but now he has turned shy. Why? Maybe he is not the company's decision-taker but hates to admit it. Maybe there is an objection still in his mind that has not been uncovered and dealt with. Maybe you didn't entirely clear up one point earlier. Maybe, maybe, maybe.

What you need to do now is to deal with the 'I'll think about it', or 'I'm not sure it's really for us', or 'I don't think we can afford it', or whatever way he wraps up the word 'No', as you would deal with any other objection: uncover it, agree that it needs attention, and then proceed to demolish it. All the time you will be summarising the points in your favour, stressing the benefits to him and comparing their towering advantages with the problem he will continue to have if he deprives himself of this opportunity. Whatever you do, don't drop the price, but keep selling benefits. If you really can get no further, he agrees with all you have said but still says 'No' and offers only silly objections, the odds are that there is something he needs to conceal to save face: one of the 'maybe' reasons above might apply. How do you discover it without making him lose the face he is trying to save? How do you say tactfully, 'Does your boss have to OK everything you do?' or 'Are you really so hard up you can't afford even a small outlay like this?' or 'Don't they trust you with purchases of only £200?' or 'Are you really that scared of your wife?' You could try 'Is there anyone else I would have to get approval from before you were prepared to place the order?' or 'Would you want one of your engineers or financial chaps to clear it before you committed the company?' or 'We've agreed that you need a couple of Whizzo-X Mark IIIs; is there any way I can make it easier for you to own? Would instalment payments help, for instance?' or 'You and I have agreed you need "Nutter" double glazing, but I never feel happy at asking a wife or a husband alone for the decision. Can I call back later and run through it quickly with you both together?' There is no certain formula for success, but this sort of approach should get better results than taking the first 'No' for an answer.

If you possibly can, get him to define what the stumbling-block is, and to agree how it is to be dealt with. 'So the only thing remaining is for Mr Brown to check it over, is it?' ('Yes.') 'And if he's happy we can go ahead and sign you up?' ('That's right.') Fine, if it goes like that. But he might say, 'Good heavens no! There's the Divisional Director to satisfy, capital authorisation to get – we're a long way off yet.' What a blessing you asked! Now you are really learning about the customer's buying and approval system. Ask him to explain exactly how they work, both the official version and the way that he and his colleagues get round them to keep the business going. For instance, he may be allowed to place orders of up to £5000, but your system costs £6000: how about invoicing the machine for £4000 and the conveyor for £2000? Could he place two orders like that without getting fired? Some companies would punish buyers severely for doing this, while others would not even notice. Your customer will know very well indeed which category his employer is in.

2.30 Pricing the product

A minimum aim must be not to sell below cost. Your management accounting (section 3.2) tells you how to decide what 'cost' is. You will obviously want to make a profit too, but competitors will see to it that you can't raise prices beyond a certain level. That said, there is a general strategy that the small firm is usually forced to follow, of high margins and low volume. That is because the small firm lacks the ability to make large investments in fast-production machinery, but unlike its bigger brother it finds it easier to ensure high and consistent quality because of the owner's personal involvement in all aspects of design, production and administration. Because you cannot make many items, you have to charge a lot for each one; and because you are able to make quality goods people will pay your high prices. One further general rule is not to cut prices to break into the market or increase sales but, if you must give something, add benefits (which usually cost less than discounts). Giving away money in the form of discounts is very expensive indeed.

There can even be merit in pricing your product higher than a competitor's. Who would believe in an 'exclusive' perfume at market stall prices? Or real champagne at £1 a bottle? Your market knowledge will tell you what part price plays; the point to be absolutely clear on is that few customers buy anything on price alone. Most buy on value, and for you that means offering extra benefits at high prices. If in doubt be ambitious in your pricing: it is easy to drop prices if you've gone too high, harder to raise them if they're too low.

2.31 Benefits

These can be of two basic types: benefits built into the product, and benefits outside it. Both are important, and to different degrees in different markets. One way of offering the second type is by introducing a practice from another market to one which has never seen it before. That can mean you have a winning combination, even though your product may be no better than other people's. Examples of this approach would include:

- *Snap-On Tools*, whose franchised van salesmen call regularly on engineers, just as the bread van calls on the grocer
- *Book clubs* who sell via colour ads direct to the public rather than through shops or catalogues
- *Tupperware*, who sell plastic containers direct to the public by party plan rather than through the shops.

In all cases they sell quality merchandise, though in a way which is unusual in their market. They have been different in a way which appealed to the customers, and it has made them very big indeed. You don't need to be vast to take a tip from their success. In every case they gave the consumer benefits by breaking the 'rules' of the trade, rather than by inventing better mousetraps. And it is probably no coincidence that they all have reputations for quality.

The examples of benefits shown below are not meant to be complete, but they do show the contrast between the things you can change with difficulty, by redesigning the product, and those you can change relatively easily. You can take it further to enable you to keep the same product looking constantly fresh, by ringing the changes on items from the second column. The final word on benefits is that they must be relevant to the customer. A no-quibble replacement is not much good for film used by a war photographer; £1 million insurance against food poisoning has little appeal to the crisp-eater.

Examples of:

Built-in benefit	Outside benefit
Better-looking materials	Faster delivery
More resistant finish	Longer guarantee
Better performance	No-quibble replacement
Needs less maintenance	Free replacement while
More reliable	servicing done
Lasts longer	Easy-payment terms
Cheaper	10 per cent off this month
Easier to maintain	Buy at your fireside
Cheaper to run	Smarter showroom, nicer
More versatile	people
etc	etc

2.32 Sales promotion

If your product is the cake, this is the icing. If you want to give the customer more good reasons for buying than exist in the product itself –

here's your chance. You might call on a customer three or four times, getting a refusal each time. But you need him as a customer. How can you give him *just* the product story each time? Certainly you give him the product story – even if he says he remembers, the odds are he has forgotten some key point. But you need something to add sparkle. How much easier you, and he, will find your visits if one month there is a free first aid kit with the product, the next month a voucher worth 20 per cent off essential maintenance items, the next a £25 rebate off a purchase of two, and the next the first year's maintenance contract at half price. OK for the industrial boys, you may say, but I sell knitwear to high-class shops and they don't go for this. Not true. How about offering to share the cost of a fashion show? Or paying for printing leaflets for them to send to their customers, publicising your new season's range? Or offering a free knitted bonnet with every three pullovers? Or lending them, free, a window display of expensively photographed enlargements of models wearing your product? All it takes is to see things from your customer's point of view – what will help him to operate better? If you constantly work hard at answering that question you will keep on improving as a sales promoter and marketer.

2.33 Selling through mail order catalogues

While they are much like other customers, they do have their own special practices which the would-be supplier must know about. There are around 30 large catalogues operated by perhaps 15 firms. If you include Argos (which prints a catalogue but also has shops) they range from the big one-catalogue firm to the British Mail Order Corporation which owns several catalogues, each with its own name.

Selling to them is different from selling to other customers in these respects: they will carry out a preliminary selection nine months or more before the catalogue is due out (so don't go to them in September with Christmas goods), and two or three months later make their final selection. To take part in these processes you are required to fill in extensive forms each time, part of which is a price quotation. In recent years it has been difficult, to say the least, to forecast prices nine months in advance, but you have to, for they will hold you to that forecast. Samples will be required from the selections, which they expect either to return or be invoiced for. If yours is lucky enough to be selected, further samples will be required, which they pay for. They usually require you to quote for transit packaging; that is, the outer pack that protects your product in the post. That can be useful if the product normally has an expensive package: you can substitute a strong brown corrugated mailing box. Equally, some products can be put in a padded bag –

discuss this at the outset with the buyer, and be guided by him. They require you to guarantee very rapid delivery of repeat orders, too. Finally, they will usually want a 50 per cent margin on sales, ie, for a product that sells at £10 plus VAT they will expect to pay £5 plus VAT. In return, you get (sometimes) massive orders, straight dealing and fast payment – usually in 14 days from your invoice.

In addition there is a growing number of specialised catalogues selling all kinds of merchandise. Some are aimed at particular groups of members of the public, others at business. They can be very valuable outlets, and all have their particular terms of doing business.

2.34 Selling by mail order

This is quite different from the process described in section 2.33. It involves you in advertising direct to users, whom you invite to order your product either 'off the page', ie, from the ad itself, or to send for a catalogue. It is a very useful method in many ways, with the following features:

For	Against
Direct communication with user	Pay for ads with no guarantee of results
No middleman to pay	At mercy of press circulations
Usually cash with order	At mercy of Post Office prices
Can reach many consumers fast, even in minority-interest markets	At mercy of Post Office and press unions
Can turn demand on or off by adjusting advertising expenditure	Results sometimes unpredictable
Reaches consumers that other methods miss	
Can operate from home	
Over time, builds up a mailing list	

Mail order can be applied to industrial and consumer goods. It works best where the product has a distinct appeal to a particular group who are served by specialist press. Anglers, for instance, or touring cyclists, or mothers of very young children: all these and many more have their own low-circulation magazines in which you can advertise fairly cheaply. There are also the special mail order sections of newspapers, particularly in the Saturday editions of dailies and the Sundays. Some special considerations apply.

First, you have to decide between 'off-the-page' or catalogue sales. If you have a single product, or a 'flagship' product with a simple, clear reason for buying, off-the-page selling may be better. If so, you will need to satisfy the requirements of the Newspaper Publishers' Association's Mail Order Protection Scheme (MOPS). The NPA were worried about the number of dishonest or incompetent mail order advertisers who took customers' money but failed to deliver, so they decided to allow off-the-page ads only after they had checked up on advertisers. It is nothing to worry about, but needs taking into account in your timetable, and means yet more form-filling. One point to watch: when you enquire about advertising, the newspaper or magazine might not mention the MOPS scheme. Check with them whether this is forgetfulness or because they are not NPA members (nearly every paper is), or because you do not need to conform. Ninety-nine times out of a hundred it is forgetfulness. How difficult it would be for you to be geared up and ready to go, and then find they refused to accept your ad until you had been cleared.

The response you can expect from display ads (where you pay for a space), as opposed to 'lineage' – pronounced 'line-age' – ads (where you pay by the line or by the word) is said to be between 1 and 2 per cent of readership. This may be a useful guide, but should be taken with a pinch of salt. Your own experience is the best guide in this field. To get experience there is no real substitute for going and doing it.

2.35 Selling by direct mail

If a name and address list of potential customers is easily found, why not write a sales letter direct to them? To service big firms' direct mail needs there are various 'list brokers' who sell mailing lists of people with different characteristics – for example, earning over £100,000 per annum, or boat owners, or amateur computer enthusiasts, or opticians; the range is endless. The small firm can use list brokers, or can usually start off at no cost by consulting the Yellow Pages. The Post Office is keen to encourage direct mail and makes various offers (at the time of writing a voucher worth over £100 is given away to pay the postage on your first mailing of up to 1000 letters), and publishes useful guides, for example, on the art of writing effective selling letters. Direct mail does offer the chance to apply some bright ideas, for you are not restricted to sending only letters. A sample of the product or a ticket to a demonstration, or a voucher encashable against the product, can be good 'hooks'. One excellent mailing idea of a few years ago is often cited: the *Guardian* newspaper wanted to get a limited number of people from big advertising agencies to a presentation. They sent invitations to the selected few, together with a couture silk handkerchief. The letter told them that if they came to the presentation they could collect a matching silk tie. Virtually every invitee came. But a bigger and less clever mailing would rarely get more than 1 to 2 per cent response. In these days, if you are mailing to VIPs, it is best to check anything bigger than a letter with the police. Your prize mailing will lose some impact if it is dropped in a bucket of water and opened by the Bomb Squad.

2.36 Selling by telephone

As a way of setting up sales calls the phone can be very useful. For example, if you sell to farmers, why not phone through the Yellow Pages list to ask if and when you can come to demonstrate your product? Be aware that some trades are usually available only at some times of the day – farmers, publicans and restaurateurs are examples. Still others are not available at some times of the year – Blackpool landladies are just not there in January, but are usually taking a well deserved cruise.

2.37 Selling by party plan

Many small businesses find this to be a very profitable way to sell. The most successful seem to be selling goods for the home or family, priced up to £30 per item.

Most party plan operators seem to be potters, knitters, wood turners, clothing and soft toy makers. Not all of them stick to the 'rules'. One haute couture clothes designer organises fashion shows in the homes of the well-to-do, at which customers can try on all sorts of clothes after they have been modelled. Her garments cost well into three figures. It is party plan selling really, but her clients would run a mile if she called it that.

To start a party plan operation you need to recruit 'hostesses' (they usually are women), the people who will invite friends and acquaintances to the 'party' to be held in their home. Normally they are paid by a share of the takings – usually around 10 per cent of the night's sales. This is often paid not in cash, but in merchandise to the value. You find hostesses by the following methods:

- Knocking door-to-door, or paying someone else to
- Distributing leaflets inviting potential hostesses to ring you
- Asking around your contacts, especially those who belong to clubs and groups
- Advertising in the local paper
- Asking people who are engaged in direct selling – the Avon lady for instance
- Contacting other small firms who sell by party plan.

The last may seem difficult to do, but the advisory agencies and small business clubs should be able to make introductions for you. The sensible party plan operator is happy to tell his hostesses about other good-quality operators, for keeping the hostesses happy and keen is important. You need to build up a good network of hostesses, because none of them can hold a party every week for you: they would soon run out of guests.

You will need to budget for two items of expenditure. Everyone attending should receive a free gift, preferably a useful or decorative item made by you and carrying your name, but if that is not possible it could equally be a glass of sherry. It will help the hostess if you give her some leaflets about your products, on which she can write the invitation to the guests.

It is considerate to include in your range a few small items that can be bought cheaply by guests who really want nothing, but feel that they do not want to let the hostess down.

Guests buy for cash at the party, or place orders and give a deposit. In the latter case, you will need order forms and receipts, which could be combined into one document. Some system will also be needed to control delivery dates, since some goods will be bought as presents for which the timing of delivery is critical. When you deliver the goods you collect the balance of the payment.

As with other direct-selling methods, it gives you the full retail price, no problems of running invoice and credit control systems, and cash on delivery. Also, you build up a mailing list that can be used for later direct mail selling, which should be quite effective as it comprises people who are, presumably, already satisfied customers. Furthermore, some of the people who attend parties as guests are willing to become hostesses.

Party planners find that they often need to operate in pairs. While someone is demonstrating and selling well, they do not want to lose the audience's attention because they have to pop out to fetch something from the car. At well-attended events, two people can be kept at full stretch taking orders. If there had been only one of them, some orders might have been missed, and one or two pieces of merchandise could have disappeared unnoticed.

2.38 Where to advertise?

It all depends on what you want to say, to whom, and what effect you want to have. If you do not yet know this precisely, do not advertise until you have sorted it out completely. Some people place ads because they feel that they should, being unable to think of any other way of getting known. Do not join them.

Magazine publishing is very competitive and this has produced one or more magazines aimed at nearly every interest group imaginable. Th helps the small firm in two ways: if you can't afford the sheer outlay o national newspaper advertising (few new businesses can), you can sele part of your market and advertise to it in its special magazine; also, yo can target your ads precisely on the people most likely to buy. So dor forget the wide range of advertising media available to you. Nearly ever trade has not only magazines aimed at its consumers, but also tho aimed at its dealers, and often quite separate ones aimed manufacturers.

The best way of getting information on this is to consult BRAD (*Brit Rate and Data*) at the public library. BRAD is published monthly ar each issue contains a complete list of all British advertising medi including every magazine and newspaper. Against each is shown all t information an advertiser could want: the advertising office address ar phone, circulation, readership, editorial office (handy for sending pre releases), as well as details which your advertising agent or artist nee to know about the printing process used, costs of ads, extras offered (ar their cost), discounts, and so on. Obviously all this is important, but yo do need to go to your friendly neighbourhood bookstall and look at eac magazine you might use.

Check through this list:

- Is it the right setting for your product and message?
- Do they bury ads like yours where nobody will see them, or do son appear with, or opposite, journalists' stories?
- Will your ad look like all the others, or at least not stand out? C will it be properly distinctive (be honest!)?
- Do long-term small advertisers – the ones you have seen around f a long time – use it? They usually know what they are doing, so t odds are that it works for them.
- Will customers instantly get some idea of what you are offerir from the sort of ad that you can afford? If not, you risk getting po results.

2.39 Buying an ad

Having decided on the medium to use you may need to satisfy MO requirements (see section 2.34). Check. There will probably be a choi of 'lineage', 'semi-display' and 'display' ads. They look like tho opposite.

The advertising sales department of the paper will send you their 'ra card' (ie, price-list). It, and BRAD, will contain strange terms like:

rop, or run-of-paper – meaning 'we'll put the ad where it suits u

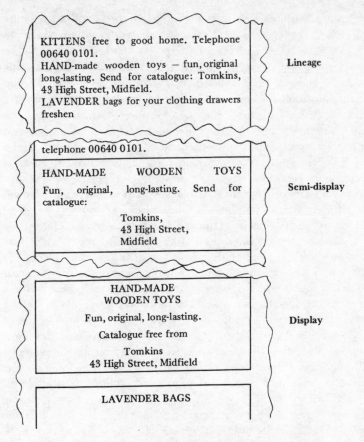

KITTENS free to good home. Telephone 00640 0101.
HAND-made wooden toys — fun, original, long-lasting. Send for catalogue: Tomkins, 43 High Street, Midfield.
LAVENDER bags for your clothing drawers freshen

Lineage

telephone 00640 0101.

HAND-MADE WOODEN TOYS

Fun, original, long-lasting. Send for catalogue:

Tomkins,
43 High Street,
Midfield

Semi-display

HAND-MADE
WOODEN TOYS

Fun, original, long-lasting.

Catalogue free from

Tomkins
43 High Street, Midfield

Display

LAVENDER BAGS

facing matter	-	opposite editorial articles, which are what most people really buy magazines to look at (except perhaps for *Exchange & Mart*) and not lost among other ads.
ifc/irc	-	inside front/rear cover - thought to be plum spaces; also covers are often printed on better paper than the rest of the magazine, so ads look better.
scc	-	single column centimetre: one cm deep, one column wide. Advertising costs are often quoted per scc.

Sometimes rate cards are *very* negotiable. Don't be afraid to make silly offers - there are many examples of people getting half-price advertising just by asking.

There are two basic printing methods, letterpress and lithography (litho), used for magazines and some papers, and a system similar to letterpress for other newspapers. Letterpress is basically similar to the child's printing outfit – you pick out the letters you want to use, assemble them in the right order, ink them, and then print. The only time you need anything more is when you want some special lettering or a picture. Then a 'block' has to be made photographically, for which an artist will prepare 'artwork'. Litho, on the other hand, requires your whole ad, words and pictures, to be made into artwork, which is laid out with the artwork for the rest of the page and then photographed to make a printing plate. This shows where the inevitable cost of extras comes from. There is your artwork, of course, which newspapers and magazines will often helpfully offer to prepare for you. Beware. You may pay central London rates (which can be extraordinary) for the work, and it will be out of your control. So when they produce something that isn't quite what you wanted, you can either accept it, or risk missing the paper's deadline and pay expensively to have it put right. Far better to get it done locally, but be careful to check one vital point with the artist: will his work be accepted by the paper? The problem is the regulations of the unions in the print industry. If your artwork was not prepared by one of their brothers or sisters in the right union, the printers could 'black' it.

In addition to the cost of artwork, there is the cost for the plates or blocks the paper makes. Best to check with the advertising sales people in advance, what those costs are likely to be, to avoid nasty shocks later. Your artwork will need to be with the paper by a particular deadline called the 'copy date'. If it is not, you could miss that issue (but still have to pay!). The paper should send 'proofs' of your ad for you to check finally. Go over them with a fine-tooth comb. Obviously you will look to see that there are no spelling errors, that the address is right, and so on. But also look for blobs, damaged letters, wrong spacing, and if necessary call for corrections. That is, after all, why they sent you the proofs.

If you start out as, or develop into, a fairly substantial advertiser (say £50,000 a year expenditure) you should look at the small local ad agencies. They may charge more for artwork than the local moonlighting artist, but they will negotiate and book space and act as common sense advisers in the confusing world of advertising. The ad booking and advice is usually paid for by a discount allowed by the media (which you can't get – only approved ad agencies can). How to select an agency? Go to see them, let them come to see you, and find out if they talk sense. Always see more than one, and don't take any of them on if you're unsure.

When you design your ad, make the *proposition* the most prominent part of it, not your name.

2.40 Measuring advertising's effectiveness

The first thing to remember is that one ad is unlikely to work. The effect of advertising accumulates over time, so that you could expect to build up to a reasonable level of response by your fifth. The man who told the author that he'd tried an ad and, because he got no replies, concluded that advertising was a big con, hadn't given it a chance. He sells capital equipment to local authorities, by the way. Advertising could open the door for his salesmen, or give their sales-talk more credibility. It was most unlikely to generate enquiries direct to him, because his market doesn't work that way. So make sure you've taken on board the first paragraph of section 2.38: get clear what your ad is supposed to achieve, and that you are not attempting something it cannot reasonably do. Defining objectives for your ads, and measuring the results, is a lot easier with direct-response ads than with others. If your ad calls for a coupon to be clipped, an order to be placed, a catalogue to be requested, it's easy to measure how well it worked. For that reason many small firms confine themselves to that sort of advertising. If you follow that example, you will quickly develop a pattern from ads in different media. One might cost you £1 per enquiry, another £1.30. But don't stop your records there – watch the sales you make to those enquiries and you may find that the first gives you a sale from every five enquiries, yet the second gives one for every other enquiry. The ad cost per sale, which is what really matters, will be £5 for the first, but only £2.60 for the second. Naturally, you could know this only where you are selling direct and not, for example, sending out catalogues with lists of stockists. Then you would simply never know which of your ads worked best. You might try keeping records like this, but amended where necessary to fit your trade:

Customer Record

Name	Town	Ad medium	Isue date	Sent catalogue	Order received	Order value
Dickens	SE11	Parents	Nov 88	23.11.88	1.12.88	£7.50
Jameson	Sheffield	Good Housekeeping	Oct 88	23.11.88	–	–

From this you will be able to develop this analysis for each ad you place:

Advertising media record
(This was not a real campaign)

	Parents	*Good Housekeeping*
Date	Sep 88	Oct 88
Cost of ad	£305	£414
Production cost	£55	£63
Total cost	£360	£477
Catalogues ordered	193	337
No of sales	108	124
Sales value	£2927	£3899
Adv cost per catalogue	£1.87	£1.42
Catalogues per sale	1.78	2.72
Cost per sale	£3.33	£3.85
Average sale value	£27.10	£31.44
Ad cost % of sales	12%	12%

Then, over the course of a year, say, you could add together the tot results of each medium in which you advertised, as a tool for decidir which gave the most cost-effective results over a period of time. If yc really wanted to know where your customers are, you could try takir (say) a three-month period and dividing customers up regionall What's the point of that? Well, there are some significant region differences, although TV culture is bringing us more together – fe instance, there is much more soap and soap powder used in the sout than in the north. Not because northerners are dirtier (one hopes) b because the hard water in the south requires more soap to be used i washing. Perhaps your product is like that, for some reason you've ne even dreamt of? Regional analysis would help highlight it, so that yc could then concentrate more on the regional editions where you sell bes and save money.

2.41 Publicity

Anyone can get his name in the papers. Journalists are hungry for 'copy as they call the words they write and, like any of us, they prefer dealir with the opportunity that comes to them rather than the one they hav to go out ferreting for. So how do you present them with an opportunit First, think about what journalists write about. Read their stories. Wha 'peg' was the story hung on? Chances are that most are about somethir new, the end or start of an era, personal achievement or heroism, the fa of the mighty, a horrifying ordeal or incident, a miraculous chang conflict, a particular slant on some topical subject – and so on. Ar active young business can find aspects of its operations that fit (some of) these categories. For instance:

- New firm formed
- New premises opened
- Business expanding – more jobs
- New apprentice taken on
- Apprentice passes exams, gets award
- Big order
- New products taken on/developed
- First/hundredth/thousandth order
- Worked overtime/weekends to get job out
- To show at exhibition
- Results of showing at exhibition
- First/second/etc anniversary
- Government grant
- New executive
- New machine
- Open day
- Etc.

Not all your stories will get printed in the form you'd like to see, but it's cheap and can be very effective. People tend to believe what journalists write – they've no axe to grind, have they? – whereas they won't swallow your advertising uncritically. That's not to say you shouldn't advertise, but that editorial publicity complements your other efforts. How do you get in touch with journalists? Note the names of the people who do your sort of story in the press and on TV and phone them. You can get their firms' addresses from BRAD (see section 2.38) or *Willing's Press Guide* in the public library. Don't forget local, national and trade press, local and national media, BBC and independent TV and radio. Assemble a list and send out a 'news release' to them all whenever anything noteworthy happens.

2.42 Writing a news release

This is not difficult, if you follow some basic rules. You need to be able to answer most of these questions: who, what, why, when, where, how – and what next? Sort the answers out into the most important (to the reader) first, and least important last. That gives you the structure of your story, and all you need to do now is write the words. Keep it to one side of a sheet of paper, break it up into paragraphs, and enliven it with quotations – no matter that the person didn't actually say the words as long as you clear it with him or her. For example:

Factual draft

Who?	Tom Jones, former steelworker, and wife
What?	Opening a quality grocery shop
Why?	Fulfils lifetime dream, made redundant
When?	Next Monday, special hours
Where?	38, High Street, Midtown
How?	Using redundancy money, bank loan and advice
What next?	Free tasting, WI demonstration.

This can then be developed into the news release shown on the following page. This example is only one of the many ways of writing up that story. Remember, too, that if the paper wants to cut it, it will start from the bottom and simply lop off a sentence or paragraph, so that's another reason to get the important bits in first.

Now a word on layout. It pays to be as professional as possible, to save the journalist time and trouble. Start off with the clear words 'PRESS RELEASE' or 'NEWS RELEASE', and the date. Sometimes you have to send it to the weeklies or monthlies well in advance of publication, yet you don't want it printed prematurely by the dailies who may be under the same roof. The way to avoid this is to print 'EMBARGO TO 27 JUNE PLEASE' (or whatever date you want) at the top right, where 'Immediate: 29 May' is on the example. Then comes your headline and the story. Set the typewriter at 10 words to the line, or so, and double space. This gives the journalist the chance to estimate the number of words in the story, and thus the space it will take, by counting the lines, as well as leaving spaces for any corrections and changes he wants to make. At the end of the story put the word 'ENDS' two lines down in the centre of the page. On the bottom right-hand side, print 'Further information from' and your name, address and telephone number. You can't claim to be a trained journalist, but you will get a few stories printed if you send your news releases to the editor (no need to address it personally) of each paper, magazine, or programme you want to reach. If you deal overseas, don't forget the BBC World Service at PO Box 76, Bush House, Strand, London WC2B 4PH, and the Central Office of Information, Hercules Road, London SE1 7DU, who do a lot to publicise British developments to the world.

NEWS RELEASE   Immediate: 29 May

New Delicatessen in Midtown

A lifetime's dream will be fulfilled next week when Tom and Sheila Jones open
their new delicatessen and village shop for the first time. 'It's a huge step for us,'
said former steelworker Tom, 'but we know there's a real demand for quality food
in the area. Other places have some of the things a good cook needs, but we've
tried to put everything under one roof.'

True to their word, Tom and his wife Sheila have stocked the shop with food from
all over the world, as well as special aids for the discerning cook. Redundancy pay
and a bank loan helped, as did advice from their accountant. The shop, at 38,
High Street, Midtown, opens it doors at 8 o'clock sharp on Monday morning. 'As a
working wife myself, I know how annoying it is to find the shops shut when I get
out of the office,' said Sheila, 'so we decided to open at 8 am and close at 6 pm
every weekday.'

The first of many events planned is a tasting of French wines and cheeses, with no
obligation to buy. Others planned for the future include special demonstrations for
Townswomen's Guilds and Women's Institutes.

Tom singled out for special praise the help he had from the Rural Development
Commission. 'Their shops specialist was a mine of information, their building man
designed the conversion work, and their accountant put together a case for the
bank. When there was a hiccup over planning permission their local committee
quickly got it sorted out,' he said.

ENDS

Further information from:
Tom and Sheila Jones, Midtown 987654;
38, High Street, Midtown.

Financial Control

3.1 Aims of this section

To survive, a business must make profits; everyone knows that, and this section deals with how you plan that part of your activity. Equally important is the need to control cash, actual money in hand, which is rarely given the prominence it deserves. The difference between the two is great, and of enormous importance. If you sell something for more than it cost, you have made a profit, even though your customer may not yet have paid you for it. Even if your customer eventually keeps his promise to pay, you cannot pay today's bills with promises. For that you need cash, and this section shows how to forecast how much cash you will have, and when. Costing is covered in a very simplified form suitable for most small firms. This section is very important, as it deals with matters of survival. If you do not feel at home with figures you need to persist until you understand it. Many inexperienced business people underestimate their costs and lose money. A very high proportion of the firms that go broke are profitable, but just run out of cash. One characteristic of most successful firms is that their managers have a very tight grasp of financial matters. Not only do they plan, but they also monitor their actual performance to see when and where they begin to stray from plan. That enables them to take corrective action before things get seriously out of hand. They also learn from their inevitable mistakes, getting better and better at running their businesses.

3.2 Costing

Sell something for more than it cost, and you make a profit. It sounds easy, and it need not be all that difficult provided you estimate your costs correctly. That is a deceptively simple statement, for while it is easy to cost the materials used in a job, it is more difficult to divide up general overheads like rent, telephone, electricity and so forth. Yet they all have to be paid for just like materials. There are umpteen different costing systems and thick books on the subject, but here we shall confine ourselves to just one method. It is of most use to the very small business where labour is likely to be the biggest single item of cost. Quite simply, you add up the cost of materials consumed by a product, add a figure that covers general overheads, plus another that pays you a wage, and you have the cost:

	materials consumed (including wastage)
plus	general overheads (rent, vehicle, phone etc)
plus	<u>wage(s)</u>
equals	<u>cost</u>

At this stage we ignore the capital outlay on machinery and tools for doing the job. They have to be paid for, but are dealt with in a particular way. To recap, materials are easy to cost. The more difficult items can be made easy to handle if they are expressed as an hourly rate for work done. The rate needs to be set at a level that should, over a year, pay the annual running costs and give you the wage you need. A costing done on this basis might look like this:

materials		£24
overheads	} 2 hours @ £18 an hour	
wage	}	£36
		<u><u>£60</u></u>

It really is as simple as it looks, provided you count all the hours you spend, and your hourly rate is right.

3.3 Calculating an hourly rate

First, work out all your running costs as you will for the Profit and Loss Budget (see section 3.11). Do not include capital costs, that is, the costs of buying things that you mean to keep and use rather than sell as soon as possible. Such things are machines, tools, jigs, patterns, vehicles, office equipment, any work done to bring the office or workshop up to scratch, and so on. Do include repairs and running costs, though. The way you allow for capital items is through 'depreciation'. Depreciation is a cost which allows for the amount of the item's useful life that is used up in a year. For example, if a machine costs £500 and will probably need to be junked after four years of the sort of use you will give it, you are using up £500 ÷ 4 = £125-worth of it each year. Include repayments on any loans you plan to take out which will have fixed repayments.

Now to move to the next stage, calculating how many hours you will work. People starting a firm usually set out with determination to work a lot of hours to get it going. Of that large number of hours, however, most will be spent selling, fetching, carrying, doing paperwork, estimating, chasing suppliers and a host of other things. They all need doing, but it is hard to share out the time you spend on them fairly between your customers. The simple answer is to calculate on just the hours in which you work productively, that is, making or doing things that you can charge for. This productive time is easy to share out because it is only ever done on individual customers' jobs. In most one-man firms it is very exceptional to find more than 20 to 25 productive hours being worked per week. The owners are often working 60 or 70 hours a week, but their uninterrupted time at the bench is only about one-third of the total. By all means set yourself a higher target, but do your financial plans on this cautious basis. Whatever you do, avoid that common problem of the new starter, of thinking that you can charge for 40 hours week in, week out, and clear up everything else in half an hour at night in front of the TV set. There may be odd weeks like that but the average will be quite different. Some weeks you will take off altogether for holidays, sickness, and Christmas, so your 25 hours a week can be multiplied by 48 working weeks to show 1200 productive hours in a year. Thus you have 1200 hours in which to get back your overheads and a wage. If we assume that you need £12,000 a year in your hand to feed, clothe and house the family, the firm will have to pay you about £14,000 before deductions. If the running costs of the business are another £12,000, that gives a total of £14,000 + £12,000 = £26,000 to be earned.

The table on page 69 sums this all up. It then goes on to work out the hourly rate, which comes out at £21.67. Do not be tempted to round it down to £21.00. The 1200 × 67p that you stand to lose comes to £804, nearly £17 a week, and the only place it can come from is your wage. The overheads will cost the same however little you charge, so it can only be your wage that suffers. Better to round it up to £22. If you are aghast at the idea of asking that much for your work remember that many firms not only ask but get it. The arithmetic cannot change, so any competitor who undercharges will live in poverty while you survive, and will probably be the first to go to the wall when hard times come. The ways of reducing the impact on your prices are:

- Keep interruptions under strict control, so that you increase your productive hours
- Work intensively, so that you turn out more in an hour than your competitor
- Use modern aids wisely, for the same reason.

In many small businesses, getting the hourly price for their work right – not too high, not too low – and making the best use of the time available, are the main keys to profit. Bear in mind, too, that 'cost' is not necessarily selling price. It is only the lowest price at which you can afford to sell. If you can get more on some jobs you will undoubtedly charge accordingly.

Productive hours
25 hours a week × 48 weeks a year = **1200 productive hours a year**

Overheads to be recovered

Family income (gross)	£14,000
Business overheads	£12,000
Total	£26,000

Hourly rate to be charged
£26,000 ÷ 1200 hours = £21.67 per hour

3.4 Cautions on section 3.3

The beauty of the rate calculated by this method is its simplicity. If you are not careful that could conceal a danger. The snag is that all the assumptions have to come true in real life. That does not condemn the method, but emphasises that you need to monitor what actually happens to see in good time if you are going off the rails. For instance, if you manage only 20 hours' productive work instead of 25, and you get only 45 weeks' work, what happens? To work it through like the last table:

Productive hours
20 hours a week × 45 weeks a year = **900 productive hours a year**

Overheads to be recovered

Family income (gross)	£14,000
Business overheads	£12,000
Total	£26,000

Hourly rate to be charged
£26,000 ÷ 900 hours = £28.88 per hour

That is a rather ambitious rate for many businesses, though not for all, but charging it may kill the firm off before it even gets started. What would be more likely is that the firm would have charged its £22 an hour, with results that might look something like this:

Income 900 productive hours × £22 an hour =	£19,800
Business overheads remain the same	£12,000
Family income whatever is left over	£7,800
Desired income (gross)	£14,000
Shortfall in family income	£6,200

This would not be a comfortable position to find yourself in.

Moreover, productive hours is not the only factor that can vary. The same applies to every item in the calculation. Too few weeks worked, overheads higher than forecast, personal wage higher than allowed for, all could scupper your plans equally well. If you use this method you therefore need to budget your costs with care, and then to keep track of each one to be sure it does not stray from target. So a simple method of recording your aim and your achievement is called for. The three crucial figures are your invoiced sales, your overhead expenses, and the productive hours worked. Overheads can be monitored on your Cash Flow Forecast (see section 3.10) so there is no point in doing it again. There is nothing to stop you from carrying out other checks, but these are the ones you need to stay in control of your hourly rate. If you feel at home with graphs and charts it can be done that way, but the simplest route is to draw up some tables like the one that follows:

Invoiced Sales

Month	Week No	TARGET £ Week	TARGET £ Running	ACTUAL £ Week	ACTUAL £ Running
Jan	1	–	–		
	2	100	100		
	3	200	300		
	4	200	500		
Feb	5	100	600		
	6	100	700		
	7	150	850		
	8	150	1000		
Mar	9	400	1400		
	10	400	1800		
	11	400	2200		
	12	400	2600		
	13	400	3000		

... and so on for the year. At the end of each week you fill in the actual sales you invoiced, and compare it with the target. You complete the running total of actual sales and compare that with the target. Thus you will be able to see at a glance how you are performing. If you are on target, fine; nothing to worry about. If you are well over or under you need to see what effect it will have on your cash flow, whether it is likely to come right quickly, or whether or not you need to rebudget. At least you will know if you have a crisis on your hands, unlike those poor souls who only realise that things are wrong when it is too late to save themselves. A similar check can be kept on the number of productive hours worked.

The last point on costing systems is to keep them under review as your business grows. As with other important financial matters it should be discussed with your accountant before you adopt any system, or before you change one.

Taking on an employee helps to spread the load, of course, so that you can reduce the hourly rate that you need to charge. That does not necessarily mean that you will cut prices, but that the chance may exist to make a bit more profit. The effect of taking on an employee might look like the table shown below.

Before you rush off to take on staff, remember that this lower cost may not come about easily. First, you will be hard pressed to do 20 productive hours' work at the same time as supervising your employee so well that he or she is productive for at least 30 hours a week. Furthermore, instead of having to find a mere £26,000-worth of work a year before the firm makes a profit, your target is now £40,000. Ways of considering this further are covered in section 3.19.

Productive hours
20 hours from owner (less than before because supervision takes time,
       and selling the extra output takes longer)
30 hours from employee (40 hour week, 75 per cent productive)

$\underline{\underline{50}}$ hours a week × 48 weeks a year = **2400 productive hours a year**

Overheads to be recovered
Family income	£14,000
Business overheads	£12,000
Employee's cost to you	£14,000
Total	**£40,000**

Hourly rate to be charged
£40,000 ÷ 2400 hours = **£16.67 per hour**

Before we leave this topic it is worth looking at what will happen if the best possible outcome occurs. Suppose the firm manages to sell the whole of the 2400 productive hours at the figure of £21.67 per hour: what will happen?

Income
2400 hours × £21.67 =   £52,008

Income target
As before   £40,000

Profit   £12,008

This is a very good position to be in, and it shows why firms want to grow.

3.5 The importance of cash

To most people 'cash' is just another word for money, wealth or riches. To an accountant, a bank manager or a businessman it has a special meaning. Cash is money that is available to be spent, that is banknotes, deposits in your bank account or in some other easily obtained form. Cash is the only thing that bills can be paid with. If you had a million pounds' worth of jewels you would be rich, but the Inland Revenue could not accept them in payment of your tax bill. People you owe money to can be unforgiving if you do not pay on time, so you need enough cash available at all times to pay the bills that are falling due. It would be wasteful to keep more than you need, as any excess could be tucked away earning interest. But too much cash, and a little lost interest, is far, far better than too little cash. If you run out of cash your creditors could foreclose and put you out of business very quickly indeed.

3.6 How to run out of cash

It is one of the easiest things to do. The most popular methods are:

- Delaying the sending-out of invoices for work done
- Losing notes of what work has been done, or delivery notes for goods sold
- Not chasing customers for payment
- Avoiding opening credit accounts with suppliers
- Going out of your way to pay cash as quickly as possible
- Buying large quantities of materials to get discounts
- Buying equipment and vehicles for cash instead of getting a loan
- Taking on staff who are unable to work fast enough or to quality standards
- Keeping on staff for whom there is not likely to be any work

- Never checking things that you sign for
- Never getting a signature for goods that you deliver
- Laying yourself open to theft
- Taking on prestige premises when they are not necessary
- Buying fancy insurance policies
- Not cultivating the bank manager
- Never planning ahead to foresee your cash needs
- Never recording performance and comparing it with the plan
- Taking a really big order, especially from a slow-paying customer.

That list is far from complete, of course. But it should serve to cripple or kill most businesses, large or small.

The last item on the list might deserve an explanation. On the face of it, a big order is very desirable. *But*, if payment will not be received for a long time after the order has been delivered, and if materials, labour and overheads have all had to be paid for in the meantime, the bank account should be quite empty long before the cheque eventually arrives. Too often in such cases the receiver or liquidator is the one to pay it into the bank.

3.7 How to conserve cash

This obviously involves doing the complete opposite of 3.6 above:

- An order is not regarded as complete unless it agrees acceptable payment terms as well as price, delivery date and so forth.
- A sale is not complete until payment has been collected – customers can be less than keen to pay you, so a few techniques may be useful: see sections 3.13 to 3.18.
- Pay your bills only when you must, and not before – it is sometimes hard for a new firm to get a credit account from a supplier straight away, so you could be asked to pay cash for six months while you establish a track record – see sections 8.5 and 8.6 on these and other purchasing negotiations.
- When you do buy supplies, buy only enough for immediate needs – do not buy 15 weeks' supply for £150 if you can get two weeks' worth for £25. Although it costs more per item, you hang on to £150 – £25 = £125 of cash that can be used to pay other bills or reduce the overdraft. This is a question of balance, but if there is any doubt in your mind, play safe.
- Avoid the desire to be monarch of all you survey, to own everything. The easiest money to borrow is finance for property and equipment, the solid, tangible things. Less easy to borrow is

money for working capital, cash for your day-to-day needs. [It] would therefore be foolish to tie up all your own money [in] equipment and then have to borrow working capital. It is better [to] borrow for the equipment, and fund working capital from you[r] own pocket as far as you can.

- Surplus staff can cause a major outflow of cash. It is fine to empl[oy] people for as long as they can earn the cost of employing an[d] housing them, but if business falls off you have an unpleasant b[ut] necessary decision to take. While you have a responsibility to you[r] staff, both as a human being and as their employer, you have a[n] overriding duty to yourself, your family, suppliers and customers [to] stay in business so that you can meet your obligations to them. Th[is] is easily said, and it makes it no easier when you are confronted [by] a weeping employee whom you have sacked through no fault of h[is] or her own; but for the sake of business survival you have to g[o] through with it.

- Avoid surrounding yourself with the sort of things that 'succesf[ul] business people are expected to have: opulent premises, expensi[ve] cars, decorative receptionists and secretaries who are unde[r] employed, and the like. Most of this nonsense has more to do wi[th] TV and Hollywood than real life. If you can work realistically fro[m] home or a £30-a-week chicken shed, why take on a £200-a-we[ek] office or factory? The only people who might applaud would [be] fools, landlords and, perhaps, some TV producers.

- Theft and fraud are obviously to be avoided, but every week o[ne] seems to read of some trusted bookkeeper who went off the ra[ils] with several thousand pounds of the boss's money. It is better n[ot] to trust people completely, but to have systems that show whe[re] money and other property has gone, and checks to make sure th[at] the records are truthful. A shiver goes down the spine of a busine[ss] consultant every time he hears the client say, 'I don't understa[nd] figures, so I leave all the books and records to X to sort out'. If [X] is a chartered accountant, all well and good, except that the clie[nt] is paying the equivalent of graduate wages for labourer's work. If [X] is simply a private person it means that the business is probably o[ut] of control and at risk of being defrauded. It is also unfair on X, f[or] if something goes missing through a genuine mistake there may [be] no proof that X is not guilty, so that suspicion falls on an entire[ly] innocent person. In another way, leaving it all to X to do is risk[y.] It is most unlikely that X will grasp, or even be interested in, all [of] the firm's key survival factors. So X will watch what he or sh[e] thinks is important, which though sincerely meant may be qui[te] irrelevant.

3.8 Why bother to forecast your cash position?·

Because cash is the chief factor governing your survival short term, it must be worth trying to forecast how much you will have and when. It brings two main benefits:

- You can foresee the danger of policies which could run your cash down, and decide whether or not to change the policy or borrow to cover the cash shortage, which is usually temporary.
- Banks feel a lot more relaxed about requests for loans if you can show how you decided on the sum that you are trying to borrow, and how it will affect your cash situation.

3.9 What makes up a cash flow forecast?

What we are trying to forecast is the amount of cash likely to be on hand at particular times. To do this four pieces of information are needed:

- What points in time we are forecasting for
- The expected flows of cash into the business
- The expected flows of cash out of the business
- The timing of the inflows and outflows.

As for timing, a business in real trouble might forecast its cash position daily. More usually these forecasts are made for month-ends. What inflows and outflows will there be? Inflows will come from loans, sales of goods and services, and very occasionally from the sale of a capital item – an old vehicle, for example. They are therefore based mainly on your month-by-month forecast of sales. Outflows will be calculated on equipment purchases, your monthly purchases of materials, overheads and the wage you draw, and occasionally payments of taxes. The list of overhead costs that you use is the same as that for the Profit and Loss Budget (see section 3.11), with the exception of depreciation. Depreciation does not involve a movement of cash, so it is ignored for cash calculations. Although the basic information is much the same, there is a vast difference between a Profit and Loss Budget and a Cash Flow Forecast, as shown in the table below.

Let us suppose that Tom is a busy teacher, but around Christmas time he makes some small mahogany boxes which are much in demand as Christmas gifts. It is now November, and he is puzzling over the difference between his profit and loss budget and his cash flow forecast.

Last month, October, he paid cash for £200-worth of timber, screws and other materials. Half of the boxes will sell for cash to colleagues from school, and a local gift shop will take the rest this month but pay in February. He expects to make 200, and to sell them at £10 each.

	Profit and Loss	Cash Flow
Sales invoices	All issued, whether or not paid	Only shown when payment expected
Materials	The value used to make the goods sold	Shows value bought when payment due
Overheads	The share for the period, whether or not invoiced or paid	Shown when payment expected to be made
Depreciation	The share for the period	Not shown — no cash moves
VAT	Ignore it if you are VAT-registered	Show it

Fortunately his accountant brother-in-law calls in, and quickly sorts out the puzzle:

Profit and Loss Budget: end December	
Invoiced sales: 200 x £10	£2,000
Materials	200
Value added	£1,800
Overheads: trivial	—
Net profit	£1,800

Cash Flow Forecast: October-February					
	Oct	Nov	Dec	Jan	Feb
Income					
Cash sales		100	900		
Sales to shop					1,000
Total income		100	900		1,000
Outgoings					
Materials	200				
Cash flow for month	(200)	100	900		1,000
Cumulative	(200)	(100)	800	800	1,800

Note. Brackets signify minus quantities.

What this shows is that Tom's profit does turn into cash eventually, but only in February. The bottom line of the cash flow table gives the position month-by-month. Before he gets his money back he is quite badly out of pocket.

Most people would have carried out only the profit and loss calculation. If Tom and his family have lots of spare cash that may be enough. But if they are at all short of cash it is vitally important that he and his family realise that the profits will not all be spendable until well after Christmas. This particular example of a cash flow forecast is easy enough to do in your head, but in a real-life business there are dozens or hundreds of transactions going on over a period of time, far too much for mental arithmetic to handle.

In real life, therefore, *cash* and *profit* can be very different things. Each therefore needs a separate forecast. Otherwise you could join the thousands of other unfortunates who were making profits, but ran out of cash without realising it until it was too late.

3.10 Drawing up a cash flow forecast

A simple example may help to explain the principles. John runs a very straightforward business selling apples from a market stall. On his first day in business he does the following:

- Borrows £200 from his granny, interest free on the promise of repaying her as fast as possible
- Buys a market stall for £100 cash
- Pays the council £10 for a day's pitch on the market square
- Buys apples for £90 cash
- Sells half the apples for £80, all in cash

At the end of that Monday his Profit and Loss Account looks like this:

	£
Sales	80
Cost of goods sold	45
Value added	35
Overheads	
Rent for pitch	10
Profit	25

But where are the £45-worth of apples he still has, and the stall worth £100? And for that matter where is the £80 we know he has in his pocket? The answer is that the Profit and Loss Account records only the sales, and the expenses relating to those sales. It could not show where stock, or cash or equipment is. The 'missing' items will appear on the Balance Sheet, an entirely separate document. The Balance Sheet pretends that you stop all the buying and selling for a split second and record where money is tied up at that moment. It also shows where the money in the business has come from. At the end of Monday, John's Balance Sheet looks like this:

Where the money came from		Where it was at that moment	
	£		£
Loan from granny	200	Fixed assets (stall)	100
Retained profits	25	*Current assets*	
		Stock at cost (apples)	45
		Cash (day's takings)	80
	£225		£225

This way of showing a balance sheet is now old-fashioned, but it is easier for beginners to understand – so don't worry if balance sheets you have seen are laid out differently. They all mean the same thing.

You do not need to concern yourself further with balance sheets at this stage of your firm's development, so we shall leave them there. The point in mentioning them is so that you can see that they are basically simple documents, to illustrate the sort of information they contain and to confirm, yet again, that profit is only one of the two key matters you must deal with. Therefore, the young business needs to monitor its Profit and Loss Account but need not worry about the Balance Sheet. Instead it pays hawk-like attention to its performance against the Cash Flow Forecast, which is a more flexible way of controlling and concentrating on the high-risk areas of the Balance Sheet.

To return to John. It is now Tuesday morning and he sets up his stall in the market again. He pays the council's superintendent another £10 and sells the rest of his apples for £80. The result of Tuesday's trading is:

John's Profit and Loss Account for Tuesday	
	£
Sales	80
Cost of goods sold	45
Value added	35
Overheads	
Rent of pitch	10
Profit	25

For the rest of the week he repeats the same pattern, ending up with 6 × £25 = £150 by Saturday night, all in cash. Having made £150, and being a nice young chap, John thinks of paying off some of granny's loan. He knows he must keep some cash back to pay for stock on Monday, to pay the council, and to pay his £30 weekly keep. So he does a cash flow forecast. He works out what cash he can expect to come in and when, and what he will have to pay out and when. Follow what John wrote down; even if it looks a little difficult at first it is not complicated. As usual, brackets mean a minus figure.

John's Cash Flow Forecast, week 2

	Mon	Tue	Wed	Thu	Fri	Sat
Cash taken in day (a)	80	80	80	80	80	80
Cash paid out at start of day						
– keep	30	–	–	–	–	–
– rent	10	10	10	10	10	10
– apples	90	–	90	–	90	–
Total cash paid out in day (b)	130	10	100	10	100	10
Net cash taken in day (a – b)	(50)	70	(20)	70	(20)	70
Cash in hand at start of day	*150	100	170	150	220	200
Cash in hand at end of day	**100	170	150	220	200	270

* He will start the week with £150 left over from previous week
** The figures on this line are also the 'cash in hand at start of day' for the following day.

The table shows that the result of Monday's trading is expected to be a fall of £50 in John's holding of cash, even though he will have made his usual profit. That profit, plus another £15, will be tied up in apples for sale on Tuesday. So can John pay off granny? Bearing in mind that he must start each day with enough cash for his outlays that day, he looks to see what he can pay granny and when. He will start week 2 with his £150 (the next to last figure in the Monday column above) and he must finish the week with at least £130 for his outlays at the start of week 3. Try working out what he can pay, and when. The answer is in brackets at the bottom of the next page. If you found that a little challenging you will see why John did it on paper and not in his head. The calculation is not difficult – it is only simple addition and subtraction – but there are so many steps to it that you cannot do it in your head. John could easily have taken the short cut and paid out of his profits. Had he done so he would have run out of cash and out of business. As it is, he still owes granny £60 but he is still in business. Having established the principle of how the cash flow forecast is drawn up, we can move to an example – in Appendix 1 – that is meant to be a bit more like real life. Although it may look very complicated, its framework is identical; there are just a few more items to list, add up and take away. Again, do not be put off by it but work through it at your own pace.

3.11 Profit and loss budgeting

The title of the document may be misleading. It would be difficult to budget for a profit and a loss at the same time. It would probably help if the name were changed to 'Profit or Loss' budget. But it is not likely to be, so please accept the traditional name. What the Profit and Loss Budget (hereafter referred to in the accountants' slang as 'P & L') shows is the sales invoiced during a period of time, the cost of labour and materials in the goods invoiced, and the difference between those costs and the sales known as 'gross margin'. It then goes on to show the overheads, that is, the costs of the business which cannot be easily charged into particular products (rent, rates, postage, fuel and so on). Finally it subtracts that from gross margin to show net profit before tax.

This may be a good point at which to remind ourselves of the essential differences between the three basic accounting documents, as illustrated on the opposite page.

If the heading to the first of these three sheets were changed to 'Profit and Loss Budget', it would represent a forecast; an 'Account' is a report on something that has happened already. The other references would also change to reflect expectations, and the last line would change to 'REFERS TO A FUTURE PERIOD OF TIME'.

When you are looking at the budgeting exercise in Appendix 1, introduced in section 3.10, one point will jump out of the P & L. There is no mention of Gross Margin, some impostor calling itself Value Added appearing in its place.

(Answer: This week, John can pay £50 straight away, £20 on Monday evening, £50 on Wednesday evening, and £20 on Friday evening. If he tries to do it faster he runs out of cash – so he still owes granny £60 at the end of the week.)

Profit and Loss Account	Balance Sheet	Cash Flow Forecast
Sales invoiced in the period, whether or not paid for.	**How much** money is tied up in the firm. **Where** it is tied up.	**Income** — shows how much, and when, cash is expected to arrive.
Expenses incurred in the period, irrespective of whether the bill has been paid.	**What** were the sources of that money.	**Expenses** — shows how much cash is expected to be paid out, and when.
Depreciation is shown. REFERS TO A PAST PERIOD	**Depreciation** is shown. REFERS TO A MOMENT IN TIME	**Ignores** anything that is not an actual movement of cash — like depreciation. REFERS TO A PERIOD IN THE FUTURE

'Value added' is what it says, the amount of value added to raw materials. It appears instead of gross margin because gross margin is arrived at after charging some labour; no labour is charged in the calculation of value added. The value added approach is simpler and thus seems to make sense in the very small firm where the exact split of productive time to unproductive is hard to tell in advance.

At the end of the year you, or your accountant, will produce a P & L account, a key piece of information for the taxman. It is also useful to you, as guidance on how you did against your plan. If you follow the controls suggested in other parts of this section you should not need to do it more frequently. However, businesses that have a computer usually produce a monthly P & L account, and if your business grows you will want to do the same. You will then have a very sensitive measure of whether you are straying from plan, as a prelude to taking corrective action.

To confirm the way the P & L is made up, you do not write down items that you expect to be charged for in the period, as you do for Cash Flow Forecasts. Instead, you show the expenses you have actually used up in the period. The electricity bill is a good example. Suppose you know you will use £100-worth of electricity a month, the bill coming in quarterly. You received the last bill a month ago and plan to pay it this month. This month's Cash Flow Forecast will show an outflow item of £300 for electricity, but the P & L will record £100, the amount you reckon actually to use in the month. So the Cash Flow Forecast for next month will show nothing under electricity, but the P & L will show the usual £100. Another steady overhead, or with luck a rising one, is the proprietor's wage. Some people might be uneasy to see that shown as an overhead, preferring to have the boss live off the profits. I prefer to do i this way because it forces us to remember that the boss and his family expect some sort of income from the firm. If there are profits over and above that, all well and good, but we must plan for the boss to get a wage in order to minimise the risk of his getting nothing.

Keep an eye on the ratios, too, as well as the absolute amounts of money. In the case of the Yule Fuel Company in Appendix 1, value added was just over 81 per cent of sales. If it turns out to be less, or more the owner should find out why. The same goes for the main overheads and overheads in total. Ratios are a key part of your early warning system for alerting you to matters requiring attention.

3.12 Credit control

If you must give customers time to pay bills, it makes sense to allow the facility only to those who are likely to pay, and to get them to stick to the agreed terms. That is what credit control is about. If customers pay late there will be a hole in your cash flow. If they fail to pay ever, there will also be a hole in your profits. The only sure-fire way of avoiding these problems is not to give credit, but to get paid cash with the order, or cash on delivery.

3.13 Avoiding giving credit

Every businessman who gives credit looks with envy and admiration at another who succeeds in getting cash with his orders. For many businesses credit must be given, but some do avoid it. Once you start, you are stuck with it, so it is worth looking at alternatives. Many businessmen will say it is impossible not to give credit, but it is not as clear cut as that If you can pull it off you will avoid a great deal of administration and worry. One advantage of dealing direct with the public is that they expect to pay a deposit, or sometimes the whole cost, at the time of ordering, and the balance on delivery. Can this ever be done when you are selling to businesses?

You probably can if your product or service has any of the following characteristics:

- *Small outlay*. Nobody really minds paying the window-cleaner his £10 from the petty cash.
- *Emergency*. If the only way the big problem can be solved quickly is to pay cash.

- *Scarcity.* The only man making something that everyone needs can get cash payment.
- *Uniqueness.* If the complete package that you offer really has outstandingly attractive features, people might swap their desire for credit for their desire for those features.

From that list, which has to do with what you are offering the customer, it becomes clear that credit is a marketing tool, and the decision on whether or not your policy includes offering it is partly a marketing decision. A further marketing point is that you can argue that cash on the nail saves you a lot of administration and bank borrowing. Therefore you pass those savings on. If the customer wants credit he can have it, but at higher prices.

If you are dealing with the public, think about accepting credit cards. They cost you about 5 per cent of the sale, but the customer can buy even when he has no cash about him, and your cash is virtually certain.

3.14 Giving the minimum amount of credit

You have wrestled with the problem of not giving credit (section 3.13 above) and lost. You now want to consider minimising it. Credit is an interest-free loan made on trust, often to a complete stranger. First, it is worth looking to see if you can reduce the sum at risk. A deposit with the order would help. This works best when you are making something specially or obtaining it to special order. The customer can see your point of view, that if he does not come back to collect the thing you could be stuck with something that nobody else wants. Anything between 20 and 50 per cent probably seems fair to the customer, depending on the circumstances. Alternatively, you may be able to use the engineering industry idea of 'materials on free issue'. There the customer buys materials for the job and issues them to the subcontractor at no charge. Whether or not you are in engineering, could that idea be used in your business? Admittedly, the main reason for it in engineering is to give the big firm the benefit of quantity discounts on materials, but it has useful side-effects on the small man's cash flow.

3.15 Setting things up to get paid quickly

Many businesses simply put 'payment 30 days' on invoices and expect that to do the trick. Most customers ignore it and pay after six weeks or more. Can anything be done to guarantee quicker payment? Guarantee – no. But a lot can be done to encourage faster payment, and it often works. The time to lay the foundation for good credit control is at the time of negotiating for the order. That is when you can find out if this is one of those firms with a fixed policy of always taking 90 days' credit. If at that stage you detect this policy you can either modify your quotation or decline the order, but if you had not introduced the subject you might not have spotted it until you had accepted the order on their terms. Usually, though, payment terms are negotiable. By asking for cash payment seven days after delivery you might get it. You will make fast payment seem like an important issue – not too difficult because it is – which will only emphasise the importance of the concession when the customer forces you to accept a promise of 30-day payment,' instead of giving the discount he is demanding. Now that it is accepted before the firm order is placed the promise of payment is as much part of the deal as the price. Thus you will have exactly the same right to kick up a fuss if the customer does not pay on time as he will have if you overcharge. Record the payment terms along with all the other details on the order confirmation that you send him.

After you deliver, invoice immediately by first class post, or best of all, deliver invoice and goods at the same time. If you get into the habit of leaving a couple of days between delivery and invoice that can too easily slip to a full week. Once that happens you will find that you have too many balls in the air to get back to instant invoicing. Customers will take time to pay anyway, so it seems foolish to handicap yourself further. Invoices should carry:

- The information required by law (see section 5.9 on disclosure of business names)
- The charge and how it is arrived at
- The date of issue, which is also the tax point for VAT-registered traders
- Any information that the customer requires, such as his order number or stock number
- Payment terms, shown prominently.

Statements are required by some customers. They are summaries of the transactions with the customer over an appropriate period of time, say three to six months. They are usually sent monthly, and show:

- All invoices issued during the period that the statement covers, those due (or overdue) for payment being marked accordingly
- Payments received during the period
- The outstanding balance on the account.

In view of the rising costs of administration and postage, many businesses now send statements only to those customers who insist on them. They can be a help to the customer in checking that his idea of what he owes you coincides with yours, and that you have registered the payments that he has made. They can help you, by drawing to his attention overdue invoices. But you can chase overdue invoices just as effectively without issuing statements, so that alone is not sufficient reason for instituting them.

3.16 Collecting money from the slow payer

This is a game that involves applying pressure with personal pleasantness. If that does not work you turn to tougher tactics. Anyone with due items on his account is asked to pay before further deliveries are made, or at least to make a firm promise of payment. Customers with overdue items definitely have no more supplies until they have paid off all items that are due for payment or overdue. Anyone who has not paid seven days after the date that an invoice was due for payment should be telephoned to check that there are no problems or queries. Customers can rightly withhold payment for faulty goods, but sometimes they are tempted to use that as an excuse to stop paying you anything at all. In fairness, it is also a way of getting you to attend to the problem fast, assuming that the complaint is genuine. In any case, by the end of that telephone call you will have identified a problem that you did not previously know of, will have sorted out how it will be dealt with, and will have agreed how payments are to get back on track: 'I shall drop everything to be with you at 8.30 on Friday morning to put the faulty one right. Can I work in a corner of your warehouse? ... Will you have a cheque in full settlement, ready and waiting?' Write, fax or telex to confirm.

If that fails you can try one last telephone call or personal visit, sounding more sorrowful than angry. You supplied the order, in good faith, on time, and as ordered apart from a minor problem that you raced over to put right. You have spent pounds on letters, stamps, phone calls, visits, interest on the debt, and lost time. Yet he refuses to pay or keeps putting you off. Your bank manager has stopped accepting excuses from you, and demands hard cash. Will your customer help you?

Because not everyone can be shamed it might not work, but if he does not pay he has only himself to blame for what happens next. Almost certainly, threats are unlikely to work, especially if he is an old hand at this game. Nor should you visit him with 18-stone razor-scarred 'business associates' and a Dobermann, or snatch goods to the value of the debt. That would probably constitute illegal harassment and theft, and could put you on the wrong side of the dock in a criminal case.

If the debt is for less than £2000, the next move is to the county court where the officials will be pleased to introduce you to the small claims

ABCD Ltd

700 High Street
Anytown AN1 1AN

Invoice

No: 217/89
Date and
Smith & Co   *Tax Point:* 12/3/89
698 Cook St
Anytown   *Your Order:* 89/2709/pr

Quantity	Description	Each	Value
8 cases × 24	Widgets no. 2050 ½"	£12.00	£100.00
	Goods		£100.00
	VAT		£15.00
	Total payable		£115.00

PAYMENT DUE 30 DAYS FROM INVOICE DATE
Registered in England no 123456
VAT no 111.2222.33
Directors: A Allen, B Brooks, C Cliff, D Davis

This is an *invoice*. It is simply a bill for goods supplied or services rendered.

ABCD LTD

700 High Street
Anytown AN1 1AN

To   *Date:* 31/3/89
Smith and Co
698 Cook St
Anytown

Date	Invoice	Value	Payment	Balance
Brought forward				180.00
18/1/89	103	55.00		235.00
27/1/89	118	123.00		358.00
3/2/89	124	81.00*		439.00
5/2/89			180.00	259.00
28/2/89	183	97.00*		356.00
7/3/89			55.00	301.00
12/3/89	217	115.00		416.00
26/3/89			123.00	293.00
Balance carried forward				293.00

ITEMS MARKED * ARE OVERDUE – PLEASE PAY NOW
Registered in England no 123456
Directors: A Allen, B Brooks, C Cliff, D Davis

This is a *statement*. It summarises the activity on this customer's account. The invoice shown above is the last one on it. The information it gives is taken from the firm's books, and enables the customer to see if his books agree with yours. Most people get something similar every month – a bank statement.

procedure. If the debt is under £500, it can be settled by arbitration without lawyers or a court appearance, and it costs very little.

Look up 'Courts' in the phone book, ring the local county court and ask for advice. They are helpful people, and will tell you how to go about it, but they cannot, of course, give you any advice on your chances of winning. For a large sum, or where a lot of argument is on the cards, you should think about getting a solicitor to conduct the case. Before committing yourself, tell him the facts and let him ask questions. Then ask him for an estimate of costs. This he will probably be reluctant to give, so you must be prepared to ask for the lowest possible figure, the highest likely figure, and a reasonably pessimistic idea of the probable cost. This is essential so that you can weigh up the costs against the benefits to be gained by winning. Ask about the chances of the loser paying the winner's costs. Not all solicitors are equally energetic and effective in commercial matters, so it could be worth asking around among your bank manager, accountant, and other contacts. Ask a debt recovery specialist (see 'Debt Collectors' in Yellow Pages) to quote, too. They can be surprisingly cheap and effective, so that it may be worth giving them the whole of your overdue debt-collection business, whether or not you could conduct some of the cases yourself. Check with your insurance broker to see if your type of business qualifies to be able to insure against these sorts of legal costs.

3.17 Minimising credit risks

Anyone who gives credit to a vulnerable customer is obviously asking for trouble. The sort of firm that is the greatest risk is a very young firm, say under two years old; the ailing subsidiary of a big firm – sometimes big brother lets it sink, accepting no responsibility for it; the customer who applauds every line in your sales story, and places a much bigger order than expected – you admire your salesmanship until your demands for payments come back marked 'gone away'; and the customer whose works, store or shop is surprisingly empty – he may be packing up, or unable to get supplies elsewhere because he owes so much. If you are selling to the public there may be similar signs – bare cupboards, lack of furniture and so on. However, unrestrained opulence may mean huge debts, so it is not an exact science. Therefore some checking is necessary.

Members of the public with a record of financial unreliability are probably on the files of at least one credit reference agency. Debt recovery specialists often have links with such firms, so that could be another reason for contacting one – see section 3.16 above. Credit reference agencies are thick on the ground, and most are better at some things than at others. Some might specialise in members of the public, others in retailers, and so on. Even a few discreet local enquiries can tell you a lot. 'Everyone' knows about old Smithy's 17 liquidations in 12 years, except you. Bank references can help to spot the out-and-out rogue. Your bank makes a written request to his bank for information, and the answer comes back in a form of words that means little to the outsider, but which your bank will decode for you. In effect, it puts him in one of three categories: we know nothing against them and they conduct their bank account properly; we are not happy with them but they might survive; or, they are very risky. Those are over-simplifications, of course, and no bank reference is infallible. Therefore back-up checks are needed. You might also ask the customer for the names of other suppliers to whom you can apply for a reference. Two should suffice, but remember that every business, however dodgy, probably has two suppliers it must keep sweet in order to stay in business at all. When you take up references it is probably best to phone at first. If they deal with these requests that way you will get a quick answer, whereas if they ask you to write in you will be able to get a name or a department address to write to. If you write, ask specific questions: how long have they traded together, how has the account been conducted, what credit limit do they allow him, and any other matters that you feel you need to know. Try to keep it short, as you are asking a favour of them, and do enclose a stamped addressed envelope. When you are with the customer, it might be worth having a form with you which you complete along with the order form. It would serve to remind you of the questions you need answers to in order to run a proper account with him. It would include information on:

- Trading constitution – sole trader, partnership, limited company
- Names and addresses of partners or sole trader
- Authorised and issued capital of a limited company, and registered number
- Country of registration of limited company
- Trade referees
- Bank branch and address.

You might use that list selectively, not using it at all for ICI, but seeking all that information, plus perhaps information to enable you to check on the directors personally in the case of a small limited company placing a very large order. Another way of reducing your risk over a large order is to offer to split it into a number of smaller orders delivered more frequently. That way you can hold back the second delivery until the first has been paid for, and so on.

Incidentally, if you are ever asked for a credit reference, be careful. The safest course is to say that it is your policy never to give references.

If you want to be helpful to a good customer by giving a good reference, stick to the facts of your business relationship with him. Do not be tempted to praise him to the heavens; just say that he has always paid you on time. If you go further than the facts, and he does not pay the other supplier, you could find yourself being sued for misleading him into giving credit. If you are asked to give a reference for a rogue do not treat it as a chance to get your own back, but simply say that you are not in a position to give a reference. That way you avoid a court action for blackening his character.

3.18 Chasing larger firms for payment

People in small firms are often frightened of chasing their big-firm customers too hard. Yet big firms can (sometimes!) be easiest to get money from. This is because some, though not all, do have a conscience and do not mind paying your bill anyway – after all, it is probably petty cash to them. None of them will want a bad reputation among suppliers, although many will feel that might is right. Also, some are badly co-ordinated so the accountant you chase for payment hardly knows the buyer who is your direct customer – indeed, they may be hundreds of miles apart, and too busy to communicate over small matters. Therefore it may be possible to chase the accountant very hard without word of it ever getting back to the buyer. It goes without saying that you need to spy out the land carefully before assuming that to be the case, but there certainly are many big firms like that.

In extreme cases, where all else has failed, you can try the ultimate weapon – publicity. Imagine the fuss if the MD sees the factory railings covered with placards as he drives in to work. His first thought will be that there is some union trouble he has not heard about. Then he sees the wording: 'XXX plc puts small firms out of business'. 'Wife, child and XXX plc to support', 'XXX plc debts unpaid for 5 months,' 'TV and Press invited for 10.30 am: XXX plc injustice', and that sort of thing. It has most of the ingredients that the media love. You might even make the national papers if you dress in rags and chain yourself to the railings, but that is not really what you are trying to achieve. What you really want is to get paid. It could well work, but it could equally misfire, by making them really determined to cause you maximum inconvenience before they pay you, and by putting other customers off using you for fear that you might do the same to them. That is why it is suggested only as a last resort, when you have nothing left to lose.

To save you having to go that far, there are one or two techniques to try beforehand. You could include in your terms and conditions of sale (see section 6.12) a punitive rate of interest on overdue accounts –

something like 10 or 20 per cent per month would be enough to make most people sit up. You do not intend to charge it unless forced to, and will be happy to waive it for a cheque in tomorrow morning's post. You might be shouted at a bit, but you might also be paid. That method can be risky too, so perhaps you should use it only on customers whom you regard as risky. More conventionally, you could write a personal letter to the customer's MD at his home, asking if he is aware that this is how his firm behaves towards local small firms, and whether it is the official policy to be deceitful. They promise to pay in 30 days, but do not, forcing small suppliers to borrow at much higher interest than he pays in order to save him from borrowing. He is aware that withholding these small sums gives him only a tiny advantage, yet to you they mean the difference between survival and failure. The long-term result will be that specialist small suppliers whom he needs will either go out of business or take on his work only in the last resort. Either way, his firm will be less efficient as a result. Instead he could have you falling over one another if he would give instructions for very small suppliers to be paid within 14 days, assuming the delivery to be in order. All very politely, of course. Many large-firm managers see the point already – the CBI, whose members include most large firms, has written to its membership to remind them of the difficulty that slow payment can cause small suppliers. So there are pressures you can put on big firms that firms in your own league would probably ignore.

Never charge interest to members of the public unless you are registered under the Consumer Credit Act.

3.19 How low can sales fall without causing losses?

This is a useful piece of knowledge, and easy to work out. You have done your P & L budget, and a nice profit shows in the bottom line. Just suppose you do not hit your sales target – should you give up, or are things not that bad? Until you have worked out your *break-even point* you just do not know. The break-even point is the level of sales that will make

	Budget		Break-even (figures rounded)
	£		£
Sales	45,000		34,000
Materials	15,000	33 per cent of sales	11,000
Value added	30,000	67 per cent of sales	23,000
Overheads	23,000	Remains same	23,000
Net profit	7,000		–

enough gross margin, or added value, to cover your costs, but not to show a net profit. The example on the opposite page works out a break-even point.

So if sales reached only 80 per cent of budget, that is, £36,000, the firm would not actually lose money, but would, of course, make less profit. The cash flow would be adrift, and would need re-forecasting as soon as the trend was apparent. Holiday plans might be changed but there would be no need for despair just yet. In case the method of working it out is not obvious, this is the sequence to follow:

- Budgeted value added ÷ budgeted sales × 100 = ? per cent
- Overheads ÷ ? × 100 = break-even sales
- Break-even value-added = break-even sales ×.? ÷ 100
- Break-even materials = break-even sales – break-even value-added.

It is worth dividing your annual figure for break-even sales into weekly and monthly figures. Then you can keep a close check on whether or not you are earning a profit each week.

Another way of showing this is on a simple chart. First, the vertical axis is set up to show £, and the horizontal to show the quantity produced (or productive hours worked, or any other relevant measure of output: usually the bottleneck factor is selected, that which cannot easily be expanded). Then the level of overheads is drawn: by their nature they hardly change whatever the level of sales, so they are labelled 'Fixed Costs' and shown by a horizontal line. Next, the Variable Costs are shown. As the name suggests, these vary with the level of sales in the business. In our example they are just materials and nothing else.

If those two costs are added together they produce the figure for Total Costs – there can be none other than fixed or variable costs in our example, and in most small firms. To show this on the graph is very simple. The line for variable costs is picked up, and put down higher up, so that it now starts from the point of origin of the fixed costs line. The last line to be drawn in is that for Sales. The chart is now complete, as shown on page 92.

We can now examine it to see what messages it has for us. We can see at a glance where the break-even point is, and how mch profit or loss will be made at different levels of sales.

A further beauty of this kind of chart is that it is easy to redraw for different situations. For instance, the businessman might want to know what will happen if he takes on a foreman at a cost of £15,000 a year, freeing him to get out on the road to do more selling. How much more turnover would he have to create to justify the decision? How bad would things look if he got only half of the extra sales he expects to get? Another application might be in helping to weigh up merits and drawbacks of

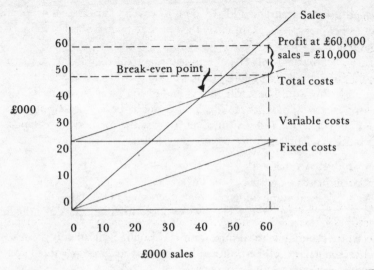

different premises. Which will be more profitable, the cheap ones that are a bit too small, or the costly ones that are likely to be more efficient? And, once again, what are the effects of under-performing? How low could sales be allowed to fall before the firm started to lose money? These vital issues are seen more clearly in the light of a break-even chart.

Careful examination of the chart also shows up one very important principle for the new starter: keeping costs variable, rather than fixing them straight away. However good your sales forecast and your estimates of cost, the one thing you can say with certainty is that they will be wrong. The best forecasts are those that are least wrong. Your worst forecasts will probably be in the early days, before experience has taught its lessons. How stupid it would be, at the time of greatest ignorance, to tie yourself to fixed commitments that may prove to be not what you really need.

In practical terms this means not tying yourself immediately to owning vehicles and machines, if you can hire someone else's spare capacity instead; not taking on leases until it is really unavoidable; not taking on staff if a subcontractor can be used, and many other ideas besides. Doing this may cost a little more per item in the early days, but it could help you to avoid expensive white elephants. The more you can keep your break-even point down, the more flexible you are. That does not mean that you never make investments in fixed assets, but that you postpone the decision until you really know for certain that it is right.

How and Where to Raise Money

4.1 Aims of this section

There is so much publicity for funds for small business nowadays that it sometimes looks as if they are trying to drown you in easy-to-get money. Of course, it is not like that really, and this section aims to offer a guide through the maze with a few warnings about what they do not tell you – unless you ask.

4.2 Grants

First it is important to distinguish grants from loans. Grants are monies given to you with no expectation that they will be paid back – a gift, in effect. A loan, on the other hand, has to be repaid at some time, depending on the conditions on which it was made. The only exception to this general rule is that some grants are given to encourage some activity – providing jobs in a depressed area, for instance. If you take the people on, get the grant and then sack them, you may be required to repay all or part of the grant.

If all of the grants available were listed and explained they would take up most of this book, so only the main ones generally found useful by new, small firms are shown here. They are:

Enterprise Allowance
This scheme offers £40 per week for a year to new business founders who have been unemployed and receiving benefit, or under notice of redundancy, for two months. Must also show that they have access to £1000, and be drawing benefit at the time of qualifying. Ask at Jobcentre.

Local Authority Grants
Many grants are given by local authorities in different parts of the country, usually tied to job-creation. Details from Town, County or City Hall, or small business agencies.

Regional Development Grants
Offer 15 per cent grants for buying *new* equipment (minimum £500 per item) or building work (minimum £5000); or £3000 per job if you prefer. Available only in Government Assisted Areas. Ask Small Firms Service (Freefone Enterprise), Rural Development Commission's Business Service or local authorities.

Tourist Board Grants
Around 20 per cent for capital expenditure on various tourism enterprises. Consult your Regional Tourist Board.

There are others, of course, so it is well worth consulting the advisory services before you start up. It is also worth keeping in touch with the grants scene as your business grows, for many more are on offer to the expanding firm. Many grant schemes disqualify people who start the work and then apply, but some work in retrospect.

4.3 Why borrow?

Perhaps this sounds like a silly thing to ask, but many firms do set up without borrowing a penny. Usually it involves the customer paying cash with order, the goods to send him being bought on credit or with this cash. Even if such a firm does need to borrow, it will not need much. These ideas are not pure fancy: the great boom in supermarket expansion during the 1960s was financed in exactly this way. If a new shop could be opened with all the stock bought on a month's credit, and if that stock turned over every fortnight or three weeks, all the stock would have been sold and the profit taken before a single item had to be paid for.

Avoiding borrowing is so important that it deserves thinking about. If you can devise a formula that works, you could save the price of a good holiday for two every year in bank interest alone.

Even if borrowing does look inevitable, before you sign for a loan take stock of your personal assets. Sell the caravan and boat – there will be no time to use them, and they will only deteriorate and lose value if you put it off. If your house is bigger than you need, sell it and buy something smaller, releasing some capital and lowering your household expenses. If you live in a high-priced area, move to a more modest neighbourhood and invest the difference in the firm. If you can couple these moves with an increase in your mortgage even more cash should be freed, but it may mean some shopping around among building societies to find one which will allow it. It will also mean a rise in your outgoings to cover the higher repayments. If possible this needs to be done while you are still in a job and can still get any necessary employer's reference to back your mortgage application.

4.4 What sorts of loans are available?

To take the banks first, because they are usually the best source – most comprehensive and flexible – there are basically three sorts of money available: short-term overdrafts, designed to cover day-to-day or month-to-month gaps in your cash flow; medium-term loans (up to five or seven years), best for buying equipment; and long-term (seven to twenty years) mainly used for buying property. There is, of course, a whole range of finance companies and secondary banks, not to mention money-lenders, also trying hard to lend. Many of these are rather tough and ruthless and are the sort of people you should do business with as a very last resort, probably only if you are in business already and in desperate trouble. Very few of them should be used if you are trying to start a firm up.

One simple pointer is to see how easy it is to borrow. If all the lender seems interested in is whether he has security for the loan, beware. If he is interested in discussing your project in detail so as to use his experience to help you and to understand the nature of your plans, that is better. If he asks for a written plan and discusses it critically and constructively with you, he is the man you want.

Why, you might ask, favour the lender who makes it hardest to borrow? The answer lies in another question: which do you think will put you in the best position – the lender who will let you have whatever you want, knowing he can bankrupt you to get his money back, or the lender who uses his experience to help you to avoid business pitfalls and to develop a wise business plan, as well as lending what you need? The former is a sort of large-scale pawnbroker, and the latter is a proper banker. That is not to say that the proper banker will not seek some tangible security, but that he will not put it first – he will see his main security in a customer running a viable company that can meet its obligations. It is not easy to borrow money from banks. They have demanding requirements which make it imperative that you approach them only with a properly thought-out case, presented in the way that they expect to see. Even then the lending is far from automatic.

4.5 Special forms of finance from banks

There are special schemes for new starters and very young firms offered by various banks. European Investment Bank and European Coal and Steel Community money is available through some banks – see section

4.8. The scene is constantly changing and it is worth shopping around to see what is on offer.

4.6 Security for borrowing

A bank will often ask for security for a loan, for if you fail they want to get their money back. On loans of under a couple of thousand pounds they are unlikely to feel it necessary. Borrow more and they will probably ask for some security or collateral. This can take almost any form, but for most people it means pledging their share in the family home. Written approval from your spouse or life partner will be needed, even if the house is not in joint names, because a few years ago a bank tried to evict the wife of a man whose business had failed so that they could sell the family home. She took the case to court, claiming her right to live in the house, and the court found in her favour. So now the banks require spouses to sign away that right in advance.

In all the excitement of planning your business, it is important to remember just what you are putting at risk. You might be able to avoid this by reading 4.7, or relatives may lend, or they may guarantee loans.

4.7 The Government Loan Guarantee Scheme

There has always been a lot of argument between banks and small business organisations over how difficult or not it was to borrow from the banks. The banks said they lent money to any viable project presented to them. Small business organisations, on the other hand, maintained that the banks were obsessed by tangible security. They said the banks would lend only to people who had large assets and were prepared to pledge them as collateral. In practice this meant that people could start or expand businesses only if they had bought a house some years ago, benefiting by inflating property values, and only then if they were prepared to put the family home at risk. This locked out a lot of people from getting into business, so the argument went, and only the government could break the stalemate. The government did act, by launching their Loan Guarantee Scheme (LGS). In effect it is an insurance policy covering up to 70 per cent of the money you borrow. The premium is an extra $2\frac{1}{2}$ percentage points on the interest rate on that 70 per cent, so that if you are paying 12 per cent interest on the part of the loan that is at the bank's risk you will pay $14\frac{1}{2}$ per cent on the part covered by the LGS. It is certainly not cheap, but if it is the only way you can avoid risking the family home it might be worthwhile. Most banks offer it as well as 3i (see section 4.8). Its future seems to be under constant discussion and further changes may well be made. Many bank managers seem to dislike offering it, partly because it involves them in paperwork, so you may have to press for it. If they try to tell you that there is a high rate of failure among businesses on this scheme, remind them of two facts; one, only bank managers ever put firms on to the scheme; and two, some banks used to misinterpret it to mean that only the worst and riskiest propositions should ever go on to it. It was *not* meant for risky ventures, just for the good ones where security could not be offered.

4.8 Non-banking borrowing

There is the good old HP (hire purchase) or credit sale agreement, of course, often much more expensive than bank borrowing. HP or 'finance' companies, as they like to be known, do offer rather more than the three-year loans on cars or furniture that most members of the public associate them with. In fact, you can borrow practically any amount from them for up to seven to ten years, but they will be very concerned indeed to have adequate security cover. Another source is 3i, formed by a consortium of banks and the Bank of England. It is interested in making investments of six figures in any sort of company, be they fixed-interest loans, equity investments (ie in shares) in small limited companies, or a mixture of both. 3i operates the government's Loan Guarantee Scheme. There are other sources, such as merchant banks, who will generally invest only to make as much money from you as possible (and why not?), leasing agreements and factoring (the finance company pay, say, 80 per cent of your invoice the moment you send it out, and when the customer pays you get, say, another 15 per cent; sometimes they take the credit risks too. They hang on to the rest as their reward). These are not always appropriate to the very young company, and your accountant's advice is needed. He might also know a private investor willing to buy shares in your firm in order to get tax relief under the Business Expansion Scheme. This is very complex, so both sides should seek advice from accountants.

In steel and coal closure areas British Steel (Industry) Ltd may have cheap money, in Development Areas the European Investment Bank can help (both are channelled through the banks) and some local authorities have their own schemes. In Wales and Scotland the Development Agencies lend money to small business, as does the Business Service of the Rural Development Commission (formerly CoSIRA) in rural England. They can also help to put you on to the right form of finance for your project, as well as giving up-to-date information on the lending situation in general.

4.9 Interest rates

There is a nasty little trick resorted to by some financiers who should know better. They sometimes quote a 'flat' rate of interest, which sounds very attractive, but it is not quite as good as it seems. Suppose you borrow £100 at a flat rate of 10 per cent for a year, repaying £25 per quarter plus the 10 per cent interest – £10 – at the end. That is fair enough, you might say – but it is not, you have been cheated. The £10 interest would truly be 10 per cent only if you borrowed the £100 for the whole year; but you did not, you paid back £25 every quarter. In other words, you borrowed £25 for three months, £25 for six months, £25 for nine months, and £25 for a year. Thus, a true 10 per cent interest on that £100 loan is £6.25, not £10. A £10 charge is in fact a whopping 16 per cent interest rate. How do you tell? Look for the small print, and if there is none (or if it is a verbal quote) ask if the 'true rate' or 'annual percentage rate' (APR) has been given. By law, they are obliged to tell you and to quote the true rate of interest.

Borrowing				Interest
£25 for ¼ of year @ 10% p.a.	=	£25 x 10% x ¼	=	£0.625
£25 for ½ of year @ 10% p.a.	=	£25 x 10% x ½	=	£1.250
£25 for ¾ of year @ 10% p.a.	=	£25 x 10% x ¾	=	£1.875
£25 for whole year @ 10% p.a.	=	£25 x 10% x 1	=	£2.500
£100				£6.25

Interest rates can be 'fixed' or 'floating' – 'fixed' speaks for itself; 'floating' ones move up and down with the bank base rates. 'Base rate' is the basic rate to which a few percentage points are added to quote rates to borrowers. Small firms normally borrow at 3 to 4 percentage points over base rate, and large firms such as, for instance, ICI, will borrow at one point over – the extra over 'base' is related to risk and administrative cost. Thus, if base rate is quoted at 10 per cent, small firms will usually borrow at 13 per cent to 14 per cent.

4.10 Other fees and charges

Bank charges are negotiable, despite what the price-lists suggest. When you are enquiring about opening your account, shop around and make it clear that you want low-cost banking as well as a good service. Query the charge per cheque, the cost of interviews, and other charges (especially if you trade internationally – a fixed charge plus a percentage for processing export documents can play havoc with margins). When borrowing money, you will probably have to resign yourself to paying any legal costs the lender might incur (eg, solicitors' fees and Land

Registry dues for registering a charge on your house) but you could possibly negotiate a reduction or complete waiving of 'arrangement fees'. At any rate, whenever you deal with the bank or anyone else it is always worth asking if there are any extra charges you do not know about. And it is not just fees payable here and now that you need to look out for: there can be penalties for not spending the whole loan after they have agreed to lend it to you, and for repaying it early. Some aid agencies have negotiated low arrangement fees for their clients with some banks.

4.11 Selecting a bank

Banks as a whole can look fairly forbidding, but the important thing to remember is that they are only shops. They rent out money, and sell money transmission and storage services. You should not fall for all the mystique designed to make you feel grateful for being allowed to talk to them.

Choosing which bank and which branch to deal with is very important. While they all look more or less the same they do have different services and attitudes. Even within one banking firm, branch managers can differ a lot. What do you need to look out for? Well, as a new starter you are probably better off with a small branch where you will deal direct with the manager. In larger branches you will deal with a trainee manager who may be very bright but perhaps does not have the breadth of business experience to be very helpful to you. The manager has all sorts of limits to observe, and if he has a small branch he may have to refer his decisions up the line for approval if they involve more than a certain figure, his 'discretionary limit', as it is called. When you shop around before deciding where to bank, try to go for branches of a size that will serve you best. For instance, if you expect to do a lot of exporting you will probably need a bigger branch, and almost certainly not one of the small banks.

Look at the range of services offered: before you interview the manager make sure you have read all that firm's leaflets on its services to small businesses in general and on any specialist services you may require. To get them, it is best to write to the bank's Head Office: not all bank managers know everything that their firm offers. Then, look at the manager – is he a young chap with a name to make, might he do it all 'by the book'? Or is he a year or two from retirement and winding down? Does he seem to want to help? Is he interested in your project and does he offer ideas? Ask him if he is expecting to move on soon, for few things can be more frustrating than working hard at presenting yourself and your project to Mr Smith only to find that he hands over to Mr Jones before your loan is agreed. It is said that some banks tend to transfer their staff every few years for the same reason as the Foreign Office does its diplomats: it prevents them from 'going native', getting so enmeshed in the local community that they start representing the customers to the bank, rather than the other way around. You will kick yourself to find that if you had asked for £19,900 he could have OK'd it, but the £20,100 you actually requested has to go to the Regional Office who will judge it more coldly than the branch manager who, as well as having the figures, also has your magnetic charm to help persuade him. So ask what his 'discretionary limit' is, the amount he can approve himself without referring it upwards. He might not want to tell you, but you can take as a rough guide that it will be about £20,000 in a small market-town branch.

Most important of all to some businesses is the question of what sort of branch they will be dealing with. Some banks have split off their dealings with business from the rest of their transactions, to the extent of creating specialist 'business only' branches. The idea is that the business customer will get a more relevant service.

4.12 Presenting your case to the bank

In section 4.4 it was said that a proper banker will seek more than just collateral or security for a loan. What else will he look for? In the case of an established firm he looks at the track record. Merely to have survived proves something, and there may even be a progressive pattern of profitable growth. The bank manager will also look for some straightforward explanation of how much is wanted, what it will be spent on, how long it is wanted for and how it will be repaid: in other words, some forecasting is needed.

Because the new business starter has no track record, he or she has to work a little bit harder at putting the case across – it is as much of a challenge to your selling ability as getting an order. You have to prove that you have thought things through and have a good chance of showing the bank a profit on the deal, or he will not be interested. At the same time, you have to convince the bank that you have got what it takes to make your paper plans work in real life. Because most intelligent people ask to borrow money that will make money, most failures to borrow are because of poor presentation. To sharpen up the presentation, some people advocate trying your case out first on a bank that you do not intend to use. It pays to talk your idea over informally with the banks you have shortlisted, taking into account any points the managers have raised during informal discussions. The paper should include brief summaries (no more than two pages on each, and preferably less), on:

- The product or service you plan to provide
- The markets you plan to serve, competitors, customers, and why customers will buy from you
- The experience and background of you and any other principal person involved
- Premises and equipment, with costings
- For the first year, a detailed monthly cash flow forecast and a detailed profit and loss budget, with outline plans for the following two years
- A statement of how much you want to borrow, what for, how long you need it for, how you plan to repay
- Security (if any) that you can offer.

Whatever you do, do not be tempted to doctor the figures to make them look good, but put down what you can reasonably expect to achieve. Getting the money is not the whole job: you will be expected to fulfil your forecast. Let the bank manager have all this a couple of days before your appointment to discuss it. If you do not feel confident in preparing it all yourself, do as much as you can and get your accountant to help pull it all together. Most of the advisory agencies can also help to do this and may cost a lot less.

Finally, do not forget that many bankers still think in terms of lending a pound for every pound that the owner puts in. Thus they are likely to be more impressed by people who have some capital behind them. But financial standing is not all. They will also judge your competence and your character. As one senior banker recently said, 'Banking is a "people" business'. By this he meant that all the paper plans in the world may be fine, but in the end he decides whether or not to lend on what his instincts and experience tell him about the person on the other side of the desk.

Your Business Name and Legal Status – Limited Company or Not?

5.1 Aims of this section

This section describes the different sorts of business constitution available. There is a lot of difference between John Smith, the window-cleaner, John Smith Window-cleaners, and John Smith Window-cleaners Limited; each has its advantages and drawbacks, and the law puts different obligations on each. After reading the section you should be able to choose the one that is right for you.

5.2 The choices available

You can trade as any of these: sole trader, partnership, or limited company. There are some rare variants of those forms of constitution which we shall not deal with. From time to time there is interest in the idea of forming co-operatives. They can be close to being partnerships or limited companies, but it is a specialised field for which specialist advice is available. Here we shall deal with only the three most popular types of constitution.

5.3 Sole trader

This is the simplest form of business, and the way that the vast majority of very small firms operate. The income from the business is your personal income, most business expenses can be offset against it for tax purposes, and tax is paid at personal rates, rather than corporation tax rates. (Recently there has been little to choose between them, but at times in the past they have been very different – and could, presumably, be so again.) Equally, the losses of the business are yours too, along with all the usual risks of business. If the firm fails you will have to pay the debts. On the other hand it is very easy to set up: there is no need to ask permission or get a licence. You just start up. Of course, there are some activities for which a licence is needed, but that applies whether or not they are sole traders – nobody may operate a slaughterhouse without a licence, for example. Sole traders and partners pay Class 2 and Class 4 National Insurance contributions. They are for 1988/89: Class 2, a flat rate of £4.05 per week; Class 4, 6.3 per cent of profits between £4,750 and £15,860 a year.

5.4 Partnership

Partnership is much the same as sole tradership, except that there must obviously be two or more partners. The key point is that each partner takes on responsibility for all the liabilities of the partnership, so if your partner runs off with all the money, you are left to pay all the business bills, not just your share of them. This applies even if the bills were run up without your knowledge. So taking a partner is a bit like giving him a blank cheque, plus permission to help himself to your house, car and other property. A partner therefore needs to be chosen with care. Even when there is no evil intent, partnerships can still run into trouble, usually because of misunderstandings about how the responsibilities are to be split, and what each partner expects of the other in the way of effort.

To reduce the risk of these problems it is worth taking advice from a solicitor. He will have seen a lot of trouble from partnership wrangles, and will be able to highlight matters for you both to think about, before the 'wedding'. He might advise you to let him draw up a partnership agreement, covering the questions that most often cause trouble, and settling now what procedure is to be followed if one of you wants to get out in ten years' time to sail around the world. If these things have not been thought out in advance and agreed while everyone is still friendly, there can be real trouble for the firm when each of you starts fighting for his own view of how things should be split. Prior agreement means less bloodshed. Usually.

5.5 Limited company

In a legal sense, sole traders and partners are people who earn income by means of their business activity. Limited companies are legally quite different. In law, a limited company is a 'person', able to employ people, buy things and sell things and generally make its own mind up about what it wants to do. It is quite separate from its owners, who are the people who have shares in it, and from its directors, that is, the people who make its decisions for it.

As a separate person, it has sole responsibility for its debts, which frees its owners from that responsibility. Its liabilities are limited to the paid-up share capital – hence the full title, 'limited liability company'. Very many small companies are authorised to issue £100-worth of shares, but only ever issue £2-worth. So if it is liquidated to pay off debts, all the shareholders stand to lose is £2, in theory at least. Yet it could have been dealing in transactions worth thousands of pounds. The only ways in which shareholders can be held liable for the business debts of a limited company is if they have given personal guarantees, rather like a parent guaranteeing a loan for a teenage child. The same goes for directors, with the additional, very unlikely possibility that they could be sued for debts incurred by the company which it could not repay because they had run it negligently. This is how limited companies are used by unscrupulous people to operate swindles. They place orders for goods which they never intend to pay for. The goods are then sold and the proceeds go to pay the directors their fees. When the suppliers want paying there is nothing left, and the firm goes into liquidation. It is then that the poor old suppliers learn that the fancy offices, carpets, pictures, tables, chairs, office machines, cars and so on were all on lease. As they are the property of the leasing company they cannot be sold to pay off the debts. As the Crown and employees have first claim on anything left that is saleable, there is usually nothing at all left over for suppliers. Done in this simplified way, it would probably get one or two people a jail sentence for fraud, and almost certainly have them disqualified from holding directorships on the grounds of 'wrongful trading'.

There are more long-winded ways of doing much the same thing which might avoid prosecution, hence the wary way in which many small limited company owners find they are treated. Banks, for example, will want personal guarantees from directors for any loan made to a small firm – see sections 4.6 and 4.7 on security for loans and the government guarantee scheme which might help you avoid much of this risk.

There are costs attached to limited companies which partnerships and sole traders do not attract. Setting the company up will probably cost £70 to £100. By law its annual accounts must be audited by a chartered accountant, which would add between £200 and £700 a year to the bill you would normally expect for the preparation of accounts to satisfy the taxman. As an employee of a limited company you would pay up to 9 per cent of your qualifying pay as National Insurance deductions. The company would also have to pay between 5 and 10.45 per cent on top, as employer's NI contributions. (All are 1988/89 rates.) In total this is rather more than the self-employed person or partner would have to pay.

5.6 Choosing which legal status to use

In the early stages of most businesses it usually makes sense to be a sole trader or partnership. The exceptions might be where large liabilities and high risks are being taken on, when it might be worth looking at limited liability status. As a general rule, however, the decision to go limited is dictated by taxation questions. In the early years it would probably be right to operate as a sole trader or partnership, paying personal income tax on the profits. Income tax starts at 25 per cent and runs up to 60 per cent at the time of writing. It is charged only on that part of income over and above your tax-free allowances. (If you cannot remember what your allowances total, look at a recent pay slip, find the tax code – which will be numbers and a letter – and multiply the numbers by 10. Thus, if the tax code is 280H, the tax-free part of your annual income is $280 \times 10 = £2,800$.) Small limited companies, on the other hand, start to pay tax on their first pound of earnings, and used to pay at the rate of 38 per cent. It recently came down to 25 per cent but could always go up again. That is a simplified picture, but it shows that as earnings grow you may wish to consider a change of constitution to minimise the total amount of tax you pay.

You must not think that the decision is straightforward: like anything to do with taxation it very much needs expert advice from your accountant. You would feel a bit silly if you took the decision without seeking advice about your personal situation, solved an income tax problem but found that you had created an even bigger problem with, say, capital transfer tax.

5.7 Forming a limited company

The usual practice nowadays is to buy a ready-made but unused company 'off the peg' from a company formation agent. They are people who make a living out of forming companies with names that have not previously been used, paying the government duty of £50 to register them, and selling them to people like you for £70 to £100 or so. They can be found advertising in Yellow Pages and in the business pages of the quality papers. Because the world is running short of sensible-sounding company names, most of the off-the-peg firms have extraordinary names. If none of the names you are offered seems appropriate, you can usually have it changed for a fee, or, to save time, use an appropriate trading name. Let us suppose you buy Quadblank Ltd off the peg (with apologies to any real Quadblank Ltd that may exist). You think that does not sound right from a marketing point of view, so you decide to trade as Victoria Cabinetmakers (with due apologies as before). Your letter-head and so on can say VICTORIA CABINETMAKERS across the top, as long as it says as well, somewhere, 'Victoria Cabinetmakers is a business name of Quadblank Ltd, registered at Cardiff no 12345, registered office 17 Back Street, Blanktown'. There are other regulations to be observed, too. Section 5.9 gives further details.

As an alternative to using a company formation agent you can ask your accountant or solicitor to set up the company for you. That could cost you a great deal more, so check the costs, and what you will get for your money, in advance. Because of the wider service they can offer your local professional advisers might suit your particular case better. They will certainly give you a full account of your duties and responsibilities as a shareholder and director.

5.8 Your business name

Choosing a trading name for your business is largely a marketing question of course. Dirty Dick's Drain Clearing might be acceptable, but Dirty Dick's Interior Decorating would probably turn customers right off. The associations that customers make from the words in your trading title will be one of the earliest of those all-important first impressions. Ideally it will be expressive, attractive and memorable. It might be right for a plumber to use his own name, to convey the idea that there is a real person who does the work and stands behind its quality. On the other hand, if his name is Leakey he might think again.

For limited companies there are rules about what they can, or cannot, call themselves. Section 5.9 covers names used for trading (such as Victoria Cabinetmakers suggested in section 5.7) but this section goes on to deal with the actual names of limited companies, whether or not they use those names for trading purposes. The authority governing these matters is the Companies Registration Office, whose address is in section 15. Most of the rules are what you would expect. For instance, a company may not use a name that is offensive, criminal, already registered, or suggesting national or local government approval. That means words like 'British', 'Royal', 'National' and 'Board' are out – unless, of course, you could genuinely claim such associations, and get permission. Your company's name needs to be quite clearly different from others, and there are quite strict rules about how different it must be. The Companies Registration Office publishes a free leaflet spelling out all the rules, which have only been summarised here.

5.9 Disclosure of business names

Until January 1982 there was a central registry in London which held records of names used by businesses which were not their own names. It was obligatory for business names to be registered there for a fee of £1, so that the people behind a defaulting trading name could be traced. That was then abolished, and the rules were changed greatly. From the point of view of the new business, the present situation is quite straightforward. If you trade in a name other than your own, you must disclose your name and address on business documents. These include letter-heads, orders placed on suppliers, invoices, receipts and demands for payment of debts. You must also display a notice at your business premises 'prominently', in a place where customers and suppliers have access. It should say:

- 'Particulars of ownership of (your trading name) as required by Section 29 of the Companies Act 1981. Full names of proprietors (insert names). Addresses within Great Britain at which documents can be served on the business (insert addresses).'

Finally, you must disclose this information in writing immediately you are asked for it by anyone with whom anything is done or discussed in the course of business. In practice it probably means you hand them a letter-head.

The reason it is important is that you commit a criminal offence by not complying, and that you might find you could not make your contracts stick. To know if you need to comply you must be clear what counts as your own name. Obviously, John Smith can trade as 'John Smith', 'J Smith', 'Mr J Smith' or 'Mr John Smith', and use his own name. If he and his father go into business as a partnership, 'J & P Smith' or 'John & Peter Smith' count as their own names: but so does 'Smith's'. If John starts a partnership with Tom Brown, 'T Brown & J Smith', 'John Smith & Thomas Brown', and 'Messrs J Smith & T Brown' all count as their own names. None of the examples cited in this passage so far requires you to comply with the disclosure regulations: if you copy the Smiths and Tom Brown you just go into business, and hang the regulations.

Now for the exceptions, the ones that must comply. Examples are 'John Smith Engineering Supplies', 'Midlands Woodworkers', 'Victoria Cabinetmakers' – none of them is the name of a human being or a limited company. Since a limited company is a person in the legal sense, it, too, can use a name for trading that is other than its own name. When it does, it must observe exactly the same disclosure regulations as real persons. Needless to say, you may not use the word 'Limited' unless you are a limited company.

Business and the Law

6.1 Aims of this section

This section outlines the main legal matters with which the businessman needs to be familiar. Because the law is such a complex area, it can only be a general guide to the main issues. For that reason, and because there are always new laws and new interpretations by the courts of existing laws, it should be used as an outline briefing. Detailed advice on your personal position can then be given by your own solicitor.

If you know little about the law at present, reading this section will enable you at least to have some idea of why your solicitor may give you particular pieces of advice. It should be remembered that Scotland has its own system. What is described here holds good largely for England, Wales and Northern Ireland. While many businesses never have legal problems, it is worth knowing the rules and limitations that bind business relationships.

6.2 Civil and criminal law

It is important to realise that there are really two legal systems operating. The criminal law is set by Parliament, the police prosecute people who break it, and the state punishes them. The civil law, on the other hand, has been developed over the centuries by decisions taken by judges in cases where someone with a grievance asked the court to settle it. Anyone can take out a summons against anyone else under this system, and the judge decides on the merits of the case, taking guidance from the principles established previously.

6.3 Civil law

Your rights under civil law are laid down quite clearly. So are those of your customers and suppliers. You could not get a policeman to take an interest in a customer who will not pay his bill, because Parliament has not ruled against it. But you have a clear right to be paid on time, which a county court would be pleased to enforce. But what does 'on time' mean? It has to be defined in the original agreement with the customer.

The court might even award you damages to pay for the interest on the debt, your costs of chasing for payment and for other losses you might have suffered as a consequence. There is a great deal of civil law, concerning virtually every aspect of our lives in the community. Mercifully, the businessman needs to concern himself with only two branches of it most of the time. To meet his obligations under them he needs to behave honestly, openly and fairly, and to act with care in all things.

6.4 Breach of contract

This is part of the civil law of contract. The only time you need to concern yourself with it is when you, a supplier or a customer, have broken it. But to avoid that concern it is advisable to know how it can come about and to take suitable action in advance.

Let us say that Johnson and Thompson sell nuts and bolts. You need some special sizes from them by 20 June to finish off the order you have from Cox International. Cox have said that they want to build your part into the assembly they are sending out to Nigeria. They must have it by the end of the month or the whole thing will miss the boat, incur extra shipping and dock charges and penalty payments for late delivery. You tell this to the J & T rep who takes your order, and he says that there will be no problem over delivering them to your specification by 20 June. In the event, only half of the nuts are delivered on time, and none of the bolts. The rest of the order turns up on 29 June, but the thread on the bolts is not what you specified, so the nuts and bolts will not match. Cox miss the boat and, after a lot of shouting, sue you for breach of contract and damages of £8000. You lose the case and have to pay up. Actually, it does not cost you £8000, for as soon as Cox sued you, you sued J & T. The two cases were heard together, and the judge ruled that you should pay Cox £8000, and J & T should pay you £8000 for breaking their contract with you. In practice, in a case as clear cut as this, no one would waste the time of the court or build up the legal costs. They might threaten, in order to get people to take them seriously, but it would be settled out of court, possibly for a bit less than the sum claimed.

If the J & T rep had only said that he would do his best but could not guarantee delivery in time, he might have protected his firm. If J & T had standard terms and conditions that specifically rejected responsibility for consequential loss, they might escape liability, and you would have to foot the bill yourself for the whole of the £8000. Unless, that is, you had such a clause in *your* standard conditions, which might let you out. The print may be small, but its effects can be quite staggering! In both cases the customer would have had to be aware of the condition concerned, or at least to have had the chance to acquaint himself with it, or it might not stick.

6.5 Tort

There are various forms of tort (French for 'wrong'), of which the one businessmen most often meet is the tort of negligence. This is also part of the civil law. Suppose that your staff have been complaining for weeks about the loose stair-carpet at your office. This morning young Angela tripped on it and fell, breaking her leg in four places. She was working for you during her vacation from ballet school, where she is a star pupil. To make matters worse, she has one uncle who is a solicitor and another who is a barrister.

By not having the carpet repaired as soon as you became aware of the problem you have been negligent, and the uncles will doubtless sue you successfully for £750,000 to cover Angela's potential earnings, pain, suffering and medical costs. Incidentally, you will probably also be prosecuted under the criminal law by the Health and Safety Executive for a few breaches of the laws requiring you to provide safe working conditions. Few small firms could survive the battery of fines and publicity from such a case, or the immense diversion of time from the key task of running the firm effectively. Even if these types of accident are covered by your employer's liability insurance policy, it might contain a clause giving the insurance company some sort of let-out. You are at risk if you behave negligently towards anyone else with whom you have dealings, and your staff can behave negligently in the name of your business: they misbehave, but you carry the can. Apart from negligence, the other civil wrongs are:

- Nuisance – eg making smells or noise, blocking people's driveways with your vehicles
- Defamation – damaging a former employee's reputation, or competitor's reputation etc
- Conversion – selling stolen goods, even if they were bought innocently
- Trespass – entering property uninvited
- Passing-off – making out that goods were made by someone other than their manufacturer
- False imprisonment – eg detaining a suspect employee or visitor who is later acquitted.

These examples of how you could commit these torts are far from being a complete list, of course.

6.6 Employment law

This specialised area is so closely bound up with other aspects of personnel administration that is covered in section 10 on employing people.

6.7 Going to law

The main aim of any businessman must be to run his firm effectively. That is usually more than a full-time job in itself, so anything that diverts attention from it must be avoided. One of the most worrying, time-consuming and expensive activities known to man is the pursuit of cases through the courts. Thus it does not go well with running a firm. Threaten it, by all means, and go as far as the courtroom door if need be, but try to get an early settlement of a dispute, even if it is on less favourable terms than you think you could get from a judge. You are then free to get on with what really matters. Remember Dickens's description in *Bleak House* of the court case in which lawyers' fees ate up the whole of the estate that was in dispute.

If you do sue, first see if you can use the small claims procedure (see section 6.8). Check that the defendant has the means to pay you – just having a big house is not enough if it belongs to his wife. Above all, go ahead only if your solicitor believes you have a very good chance of winning.

The best way of not getting to court, as plaintiff or defendant, is to ensure that all your buying and selling is carried out in such a way that both sides understand what is offered and what is promised, and to have documentary proof, and to deal honestly. In that way you can enrich yourself rather than the lawyers. Even where friends and relations are concerned (or perhaps especially then), you should have written agreements and written records of transactions and undertakings.

6.8 Suing in the county court, and being sued

If you believe you have a claim against someone you can usually pursue it in the county court. For large sums and complex cases you would be well advised to do so only with the help of a solicitor, so it could cost a great deal of money, especially if you lose. Even if you win, you could find that you are awarded damages but not your legal costs of professional help. If your costs are high enough, it is quite possible that the whole affair will have lost you money. Recognising the injustice of this, the powers that be invented the 'small claims procedure'. Under this, a claim for £500 or less will automatically go to arbitration first, and in fact clears up most cases without the need for solicitors or for a full court hearing.

Arbitration is an informal procedure and less complicated than a full court hearing, being designed to enable ordinary people to seek justice without the need to pay for legal representation. Both sides fill in simple forms and then meet the arbitrator, who is usually himself a solicitor, and each other, sitting round a table, in private. The court officials will help with advice on procedure and can give you a very readable booklet which explains things simply and clearly. No business should be without a copy, for it also tells you what to do if someone sends you a summons. Your local county court can be found under 'courts' in the phone book.

Most small firms will come across this procedure on the rare occasions when they have to take a slow-paying customer to court to get paid, when no other part of the contract is in dispute. Anything more complex is not for the 'do it yourself' method, but needs proper, professional advice. Whatever you do, do not try to pursue a complicated matter yourself, get into a mess, then go to a lawyer to unscramble the mess. Solicitors do not come cheaply – £30 to £50 an hour is not uncommon – but the good ones are usually worth it. By the way, another fascinating difference between Scotland and the rest of us: in Scotland some solicitors are called 'Writer to the Signet', a charming and dignified title.

6.9 Buying and selling goods

This central part of a firm's activity is governed by various pieces of parliamentary legislation, as well as by the civil law of contract and tort. Under section 6.4 we looked briefly at one example of how the law of contract could affect a firm. In case the law looks as if it will involve you in worry and expense day after day, things need to be put in proportion. It is almost enough to say that you will never have a brush with the law, civil or criminal, if you:

- Tell the truth
- Never make promises you cannot keep
- Keep the promises you make
- Know what your obligations are and keep to them
- Know and observe your customers' rights
- Behave fairly and reasonably
- Can prove what you say is true
- Read and understand what you are signing
- Make proper use of professional and official advice.

To help towards this, the following parts look at some of the main details that you need to understand.

6.10 What makes a contract

For a contract to be made three things must be present:

- *Offer*. That is to say, someone has to start the ball rolling by offering something for sale.
- *Acceptance*. Someone else has to accept the offer.
- *Consideration*. There must be a payment of some kind, not necessarily money, in exchange.

A contract can be made on specified terms, like delivery within a week but payment in two months' time. It also has 'implied terms' that do not need to be spelled out but are automatically a part of every contract struck. These are dealt with in section 6.13. For practical purposes the contract exists and is legally enforceable the moment the agreement is reached over what is offered and what the price will be. It is then too late to ask for changes. It does not affect the legal rights of the matter if it is not in writing, but it may be a lot easier to prove what was agreed if it is written and signed. The only common exceptions to this rule are land sales in England, Wales and Northern Ireland which must be written contracts, and in those special cases where the customer is allowed time to change his mind if he wants to. An example of this is when the customer makes a contract in his home – section 6.20 gives details.

6.11 Terms and conditions: buying

One day you order some goods from a sales rep. He writes the order down and gives you a carbon copy. Instead of that, or in addition, an acknowledgement of your order may arrive a few days later from his head office. You might do no more than glance at it to check that they have got the quantity, price and delivery date right, and file it. Beware! You might just have taken a time bomb on board. On the back are some densely printed terms and conditions, which nobody ever bothers to read. If you did read them, assuming they were not written in incomprehensible legalese, you would quickly see that they say, more or less, 'we can do whatever we like about your order and you have no come-back'. While that sounds too one-sided for comfort, perhaps it does not really matter.

Perhaps it does. Suppose that you need 200 three-foot strips of wood. Your supplier operates in metric, and sells two-metre lengths. Therefore you order 100 two-metre strips from him. Allowing for the 5 per cent you know you will waste, that will enable you to get the 200 three-foot lengths that you need. But when you read their terms and conditions you find that they reserve the right to measure length with a 10 per cent variation. Some, or even all, of the wood could be about six feet long when it is delivered, too short for two three-foot lengths *and* 5 per cent waste. And yet you might still have to pay for it. If all you had told the rep was that you wanted 100 two-metre lengths, hard luck, especially if you had a copy of their catalogue or price list stating their standard terms and conditions. By placing the order on those terms, you had implicitly accepted all their small print. On the other hand, if you had made it clear to the rep that what you really wanted were the three-foot strips plus 5 per cent for waste, and asked him to supply timber that would fit the bill, you would be under no obligation to pay for the strips that were too short to use. So the first rule is to specify what you want the goods to do, as part of placing the order. The next thing is to issue an official order which you can marry up with the invoice when it comes in, for checking. Your official order has on it your terms of trade, which might say, in effect, 'we are in the right, even when we are wrong'. Those terms would stick if the seller did not send an acknowledgement of order. The rule here is that the last one in wins. So make sure that you buy on your terms, not someone else's, wherever possible. This sort of carry-on does sound childish, but some suppliers' orders do seem to license them to please themselves about how much they send you and when, as well as to vary colour, size, weight, and more besides. Even if the rep promised you that a particular condition would not apply in your case, it is almost certain that somewhere the conditions say he has no authority to promise that.

The small print usually also tells you how to complain if the goods are delivered damaged or are in some other way not what you ordered. Leave it too long, or register your complaint in the wrong way (eg by phone instead of recorded letter), and they might still be able to make you pay. Fortunately most firms, and certainly the big public companies, are mainly interested in having satisfied customers. But remember that their small print did not get there by accident.

6.12 Terms and conditions: selling

This should definitely not be seen as a chance to hit back for all the indignities that suppliers try to impose on you in *their* small print. It is better to see this as part of your marketing stance, an effort to communicate your reasonable expectations and requirements of your customer. As such it will be written in clear language, although it must give you adequate legal protection. To give you a start in preparing your own, a draft set of terms and conditions appears below. It is not there to suggest that there is only one approach, nor that this approach is perfect. It is offered as something to think about and to change into a form suitable for your business. When that has been done you should give it to your solicitor for his comments, to make sure that the final form is legally enforceable and covers what your firm should cover. Remember, too, that the conditions must be part of the 'offer', that is, the customer could reasonably have been expected to know about them before placing the order.

Because you are more interested in having happy customers than in having rows in which you can prove you are in the right, you will probably want to make quite sure that your customers have seen them. They could be displayed, prominently marked, at your place of business, as well as printed in catalogues and price-lists, and attached to or printed on the back of order forms, confirmations and so on. If you do print them on the back, it is only fair to the customer to draw his attention to them. This could easily be done by means of a notice on the front of the document. Each numbered clause in the list below has comments after it, explaining why it is suggested.

Terms and conditions of sale
1. Descriptions shown in brochures, advertisements, and by way of samples are correct at the time of going to press, errors and omission excepted. They are liable to alteration at any time without notice.
   This is meant to protect you from minor complaints about changes in specification, and mistakes in price-lists and catalogues. You might want to change a specification but not throw away catalogues. But it would not override the customer's right to goods that are 'fit for use' – see section 6.13.
2. We may revise prices without notice. Prices will be those ruling at the date of despatch. Any invoice query should be made in writing within ten days of the date of the invoice. All prices exclude VAT which is due at the rate currently in force. Quotations and estimates remain current for one month.
   Some protection against cost-increases that you might have to pass on. Stops you being bound by old quotations. Makes it clear that VAT has to be paid.
3. All accounts are payable in full within four weeks of invoice date.
   Or whatever your terms are – very important to specify clearly.
4. We cannot accept liability for delay in despatch or delivery.
   It is not your fault if the Post Office loses the parcel for a month.
5. Orders for goods may be cancelled only with the written agreement of one of our directors. Orders for goods made to special order cannot be cancelled.
   Only a director or the owner should give this permission, not salesmen or others. Special orders are usually unsaleable to anyone else.
6. All orders over £100 will be delivered free within 10 miles. Elsewhere, carriage may be charged in addition to the quoted price.

Orders for less than £100 are not normally accepted for a credit account.

Whether you charge for delivery and what you charge needs to be carefully controlled, as does the cost of administering a lot of small accounts. There is nothing special about £100; it is just an illustration.

7. Shortage of goods or damage must be notified by telephone within three days of delivery, and confirmed in writing within seven days of delivery, or no claim can be accepted. Delivery of obviously damaged goods should be refused. Notifications should give delivery note number, a list of quantities of the products damaged, and details of the type of damage. Damaged goods must be retained for inspection.

This should be written in the light of what your carrier's conditions say. As he destroys all papers proving delivery after a short time, he wants you to notify him quickly of any claim. It is essential for damaged goods to be saved and eventually collected by you to stop dishonest collusion between customers and lorry-drivers, and multiple claims against one damaged item.

8. Liability cannot be accepted for non-delivery of goods if written notification is not received within ten days of the date of invoice.

See comments on 7 above: tie in with carrier's conditions.

9. No liability is accepted for any consequential loss or damage whatsoever, however caused.

In cases of extreme negligence by your staff or yourself this would probably not stick, but your solicitor might want to see it included.

10. Acceptance of the goods implies acceptance of these conditions. These conditions may not be varied except in writing by one of our directors.

Now the customer cannot take the goods but complain about the conditions. Nor can he bully your salesman into giving unlimited credit, for instance.

11. Under some circumstances we may cancel the contract without notice or compensation. Such circumstances would include inability to obtain materials, labour and supplies, strikes, lockouts and other forms of industrial action or dispute, fire, flood, drought, weather conditions, war, civil disturbance, act of God or any other cause beyond our control making it impossible for us to fulfil the contract.

Cover for the times when snow blocks the roads and so on. You might even want to add the insurance policy favourites of damage by aircraft, falling trees, radioactive and biological hazards ... but, there again, you might not.

12. Until they have been paid for we reserve our title in goods supplied.

When a customer goes into liquidation everything in his possession is sold to pay the creditors, even if it has not been paid for. The exceptions are items on lease or hire purchase, or that clearly belong to somebody else. You cannot snatch back the last delivery you sent him. Clause 12 gives you protection, by saying that they remain yours until paid for. You could show the liquidator this term on the copy of the order form signed by the customer, and walk out with the goods. It will not work, however, if what you supplied has been incorporated in something else. Nor will it work if you cannot identify those items as precisely the ones on the invoice.

13. Any invoice not paid in full by the due date shall attract interest payments. These will accrue from the due date at the rate of 10 per cent per month.

    Unless you have a licence to offer credit you must not charge the public an interest rate, and one this high would almost certainly be disallowed. It is suggested that you think about using a clause like this to encourage payment in line with your terms. You would probably never need to actually charge it as the threat would be enough to make most firms pay up. Any customer who queries it can be told that it does not apply to him, but to people who break their promise to pay on time. Some firms use a figure of 20 per cent, but this might be so high as to break the rules that the terms must be 'reasonable'. At 10 per cent you might be able to argue reasonableness, as it would compensate for the management time spent chasing overdue debts. What is reasonable will depend to a great extent on the nature of your particular business.

14. If a 'quotation' is given it is a firm price for the job but subject to these terms and conditions. An 'estimate' is our best estimate of the final cost but may be subject to fluctuation due to the exigencies of the job which may be difficult or impossible to foresee.

    In some businesses it is difficult to give a price for some work, as time may have to be spent to uncover the root of the problem before a proper quotation can be given. It is fair to the customer and yourself to make this clear.

This is only a list of suggestions. Some may be right for your business, others wrong, and some right after rewriting. Yet others may be needed that do not appear there. Use the list to build your own conditions of sale that reflect the way you want to deal with your customers. Then, and very importantly, let your solicitor put it into proper shape.

6.13 Conditions and warranties

In any contract there are 'conditions' and 'warranties'. Conditions are really important matters, so that if one party breaches them the other is entitled to his money back, plus damages. Warranties are less important, entitling the injured party to damages only. These can be spelled out, in price, delivery date, quantity, and the matters dealt with in section 6.12. In addition, there are implied conditions which do not have to be spelled out, but are present in all contracts. They include:

- Seller has the right to sell; (the goods are not stolen, or on HP, for example)
- Goods comply with description; (if reconditioned, not described as new etc)
- Goods are of 'merchantable quality' and 'fit for use' in the way the customer expected; (they must do what is reasonably expected of them. A pruning knife will cut quite thick stems, but not fall open in your pocket and gash your hand. A car must go, steer and stop. If you advise the customer that something will do a particular job it must be capable of it. The only exceptions are where the customer carries out the sort of examination of the goods that could reasonably be expected to throw up the fault, or where you point it out to him. If the pruning knife does misbehave in the way described, the maker may have been negligent. This brings us into the realms of 'product liability', so far not a vitally important area for domestic firms, but those selling in the USA must take professional advice on it. If it is not insured against they face amazing risks. It is likely to become more significant throughout the EC in the future).
- Sample corresponds with bulk; (assuming the buyer gets a chance to check the sample you supplied against the full delivery, and that the bulk did not conceal some fault that reasonable inspection should have shown, then the sample must be representative).

Thinking of all the legal fees that must have changed hands through the years on arguments over the meaning of words, one wonders if 'reasonable' might not have earned more for the legal profession than most. It is so open to interpretation that it emphasises the need in all your dealings, buying as well as selling, to agree exact specifications with customer or supplier. It is not always possible, but can be done more often than not. The customer wants 'a good, sturdy table' – get him to look at some pieces of wood and specify the thicknesses and type of timber he wants. He wants his gates 'rustproofed' – does that mean metal sprayed, hot-dip galvanised, or a coat of red oxide primer? Does he want you to explain the different costs and performances? Now he can really tell you want he wants, you get a reputation for being helpful, and the area for possible misunderstanding is reduced.

6.14 Guarantees

In your trade it may be common for manufacturers to give written guarantees with their products that you build into your goods. That is helpful of them, but it does not relieve you of any of your obligations.

Whoever supplies the faulty goods is the person whom the customer can demand satisfaction from, whether or not he was the manufacturer. You must therefore put right the customer's problem at your expense, and then chase the manufacturer to put right your complaint against him. In practice, you might seek satisfaction from your supplier, but whether or not you get it does not affect your obligation to the person who bought from you.

Another important point is that the customer's rights against the supplier do not have a time limit – except what is 'reasonable' in the circumstances.

6.15 Exemptions

It is a criminal offence to try to deprive customers, whether trade or public, of their legal rights. Thus the shops may no longer display signs saying 'No refunds on Sale goods', or 'No guarantees with special offers'. Sales to business customers may be subject to 'reasonable' exclusion clauses, but not sales to the general public. This also applies to goods hired, rather than sold. An exclusion clause may be reasonable under certain conditions, among them being the question of a discount being given in exchange. Much more complete details appear in a free leaflet published by the Department of Trade and Industry which can be got direct from them or from Citizens' Advice Bureaux, Small Firms Centres and Chambers of Commerce. It is called 'A Trader's Guide – law relating to the supply of goods and services'.

6.16 Trade descriptions

To comply with this legislation you have to be sure that what you say about what you sell is true, and the whole truth. 'Leather shoes' is a wrong description if the uppers and soles are leather but the linings are plastic. 'Hand made' is either true or untrue, although the Trading Standards Office may be lenient if such a product had a modest amount of insignificant machine work. It is not necessary to go to ludicrous lengths to avoid an offence. A cardigan might contain wool grown in Australia, dye made in Germany, and buttons made in Hong Kong from American plastics. As long as it was knitted and made up in the UK it counts as made here.

6.17 Consumer credit

A customer might ask you the favour of letting him pay you off over a period of time. By doing so you might break the Consumer Credit Act.

If you think you might need to offer the public some sort of credit facility check with your solicitor how to go about it properly. If your problem is that your customers do not need to pay you off over a period of time, just that they do not always have enough money on them when they see you, you can accept cheques backed by guarantee cards for transactions of up to £50, and credit cards like Access and Visa for larger amounts. Your bank manager will tell you what the procedures are.

6.18 Trading Standards Officers

Mention has been made of these officials who are the successors to the Weights and Measures Officers. As the name suggests, they are employed to enforce the various Acts of Parliament that affect trading. Before you start trading it is an excellent idea to ask for an appointment to meet one to talk over your proposed business and get his advice on what the law will require you to do. They are most helpful, and much prefer to see that you avoid committing an offence rather than catch you when you do. They work for county councils and metropolitan authorities or their successors. The only snag is that because their area is local, the advice may only be a local interpretation of the law. If a local officer in another part of the country sees things differently from the one nearest to home, it will do you no harm to be able to show that you were acting in good faith, and on the advice of one of his professional colleagues.

One way in which their advice can be particularly valuable is over the labelling of goods. If you sell products in some form of package there are almost certainly very detailed regulations about what the label may and may not say, what must be disclosed, what units of measure may be used (imperial/metric, volume/weight), what abbreviations are permitted, what size of letters must be used – and so on. The Trading Standards Officer will be pleased to explain it all and tell you where you can get your own copy of the regulations concerned.

6.19 Copyright, registered designs and trade marks, and patenting

The law gives some protection to your brand names and any devices you may have developed. Certain types of protection can be costly, and the protection given less than expected. Suppose you spend around £5,000 to £10,000 over the three or four years it takes to get a full patent. You expect that to more or less guarantee immunity from copyists. But what happens if someone does copy you? In theory, the law is on your side but you need to be pretty well-heeled to risk a lawsuit. You may be in the right but you cannot afford to prove it, unless you had the foresight to insure for the legal fees for defending it. Fortunately, cynical copying of a patented thing is rare, and there are in any case other types of protection available.

The least protection is given at lowest cost by copyright. You automatically have copyright in anything original on paper – drawings, music, names, words, writing and so on. The protection also includes anything made from copyright drawings. The trouble is that all the copyist has to do to get away with it is to avoid copying a substantial part of your work. Because the near-copy will itself be original it will itself have copyright. To try to frighten the copyist off an item on paper you can put a ©, your name and the date on it. At least it shows you are aware of your rights. If you want to be really careful you can sign and date every drawing, including back-of-envelope sketches, and keep them safely. You can establish the truth of the date you claim by sealing the papers in an envelope and posting it to your bank or solicitor to keep unopened. The postmark is your proof, but you will need to make arrangements with the keeper to make sure the envelope is not opened by mistake.

If you invent a new name for a product you can stop others from using it by registering it at the Trade Marks Registry. You can also search their records to make sure it really is original. There are agents who will do this for you. Whether you do it yourself or use an agent, think up at least half a dozen names you could possibly use in case your first choice is already registered. Registering your own mark will cost at least £100 through an agent. Unfortunately registration is not foolproof as it is not compulsory for trade marks to be registered. Many which have been established through long use have never been registered but their users have powerful claims to stop you from using them. Much the same arrangement applies to registered designs, which give broader protection than copyright but less than patents. Patents are much more complex and costly, but stitch up your rights more clearly. Registration and patents need the expert services of a patent agent – look them up in the Yellow Pages and shop around for quotes.

The whole principle of patenting something revolves around proving that you were the first with it. Therefore it is vital to take advice from a professional before anyone else is told anything. This applies to possible customers and suppliers, friends you might talk it over with, the draughtsman who might do the drawings, or anyone who might see the prototype. If you have 'disclosed' it in any way your rights may be nullified. The agent will probably advise an initial application, which is simpler and cheaper than a full application but can still run out at several hundred pounds. That establishes your place at the head of any queue, and gives you a year in which you can work up prototypes and try to find buyers. If it then looks commercially viable you can go ahead with a full patent, but if not you can drop it at less cost. The protection does not last for ever.

The life of a copyright in 'artistic' products is the life of the author plus 50 years; but if that copyright work is the basis of an industrial design, protection runs for 15 years from the first time the product is put on sale.

Designs are protected from the date of application for registration for 15 years, provided the registration is renewed every five years. Patents give 20 years' protection from the date of filing the first specification at the Patent Office.

Insurance against legal fees was mentioned earlier. Even for fairly routine work lawyers seem to charge a lot. In the specialised field of patent work the costs of proving infringement can be astronomical. Special insurance policies are available to cover these costs, which are a must for any small-business owner of a patent. Anyone who might be tempted to risk copying a patented article owned by Joe Bloggs would quickly pull back if he got a letter from a large insurance company's lawyers demanding that he stop. Joe Bloggs is one thing, Intergalactic Mutual Insurance is quite another.

6.20 Doorstep selling – the 'cooling-off' period

Under some circumstances members of the public who buy in their own homes or at their work place have the right to cancel an order, an HP or a credit sale agreement. The law was framed to protect easily-swayed people from their enthusiasms, and it is important to draw it to the customer's attention in the correct way. It also applies if you do not normally sell in customers' homes, but the customer takes the order form etc away 'to think about it' and signs it there. The Office of Fair Trading publishes leaflets which are available from Trading Standards Offices and Citizens Advice Bureaux.

Premises

7.1 Aims of this section

Many new businesses need to take on their own premises straightaway, others can work from home initially but need to move out later, and some never need specialised premises at all. Land and buildings can cause legal and other problems, but, as always, a little preparation can save a lot of trouble later. This section deals with working from home, the planning permission system, and the main matters to do with finding and renting a workshop.

7.2 Can you work from home?

A surprising number of business start this way. The main thing they have to fear is action by the local authority to close them down, usually sparked off by a complaint from a neighbour. If no one complains the local authority will usually turn a blind eye, as long as the firm does not provoke action – by burning rubbish, making noise or parking the hulks of old cars on the front lawn, for instance. Therefore this can usually be done successfully only for as long as you give nobody cause for complaint.

Some people may be disturbed by the idea of 'industry' getting a toehold in a residential area (and who can blame them?), and might complain to stop the precedent being established, even though you have been a model neighbour. A few are the jealous, twisted types who will complain about anything if it will spread a little misery. This is why many firms keep their activity completely secret. They whitewash the inside of the garage windows and never open the doors when anyone is about. The children's bikes are kept in a garden shed, to save neighbours' children from seeing inside the garage. Their families are briefed on what answers to give to the inevitable questions. Common sense tells them to work quietly, not to let visitors park across neighbours' driveways, to go out to fetch materials rather than have them delivered on lorries, not to store things outside, nor run unsuppressed electric motors during evening TV, or in any other way to be a bad neighbour. Above all, the sensible ones never allow their commitment to establishing the firm to get in the way of remembering that most people do not want to live next door to a busy factory, and even consider soundproofing the inside of the workshop.

If you decide to work like this, never drop the high standards of behaviour you start off with. Your neighbours are not all fools and some will get a shrewd idea of what is really going on. If you feel that they can be trusted, you might therefore confide in them at the outset. Do not feel that the absence of trouble for the first three months means that you can now start to store things in the garden to make more room in the workshop. Do not forget that what you are doing is not legal, and that you are vulnerable all the time. What may be, from your point of view, a small, neat, unobtrusive stack of material in the garden may look to a neighbour like the thin end of a wedge that will turn the whole area into little better than a rubbish dump. Fortunately, you have friends in high places.

Some time ago the government recognised that many small businesses can be run from home without upsetting anyone, and therefore instructed local authorities to stop closing down such activities purely on principle. They can still be stopped from operating if they are nuisances. If the local authority wishes you to stop it will probably ask you to apply for planning permission, which is dealt with in section 7.5. If you can possibly work from home it will pay you to do so, not only from the point of view of rent and rates but also because you can work hours you would normally spend travelling. Because you may need to incur the expense of legitimate premises at some time you should cost into your overheads the sort of rent and rates you would have to pay outside. By doing that you will avoid a sudden jump in prices when you do eventually move out. Development agencies and enterprise agencies might support your cause with the local authority.

It is vital that you inform your insurers that the house is being used for business, otherwise some exclusion clause may operate if the house burns down. If you are buying the house on mortgage, the firm that lent the money should be told. As with other important communications these notifications should be in writing with a copy for your files. If your property is rented it would be worth asking your solicitor about telling the landlord. You do not want to be told to stop, but you might risk a claim from him if what you are doing invalidates his insurance.

Your solicitor should also be asked about restrictive covenants operating on the property. Not only could they affect your right to work from home, but they might affect the attitude of the organisation that holds the mortgage.

Needless to say, because of the obvious insecurity of premises without planning permission, only the bare minimum should be invested in making them usable.

7.3 Availability of small workshops

Many young firms expect to be able to find a cheap and cheerful workshop fairly easily. Unfortunately, due partly to the redevelopment of many old areas, and the planning control policies of the 1960s, there is a great shortage of them in many areas. Recently a lot of brand-new workshops have been built in the 500 to 2000 sq ft range both by local authorities and in response to tax incentives. Owing to the high cost of building they have to be let at higher rents than many new businessmen expect.

In some country areas there may be the chance of using an old barn or some other redundant building, but do not be surprised if you have to persuade the local planning authority to allow you to use the one you have your eye on. Because of this it is important to start the search for premises long before you think it is necessary. Here one of the development agencies may be able to help the rurally based firm: some even give grants to encourage it. The Rural Development Commission's Business Service is expert on these matters. Even then, town or country, you might have to settle for what is available rather than what is affordable. Remember too that walls and a roof are only a start. Necessary – and costly – extras include water, drains, electricity, gas, vehicle turning and parking space, road access and security measures.

7.4 Finding a small workshop

Estate agents are the obvious people to approach first. Be sure that they keep you on their mailing lists, and get as much information as you can on rent, rates and availability. Unfortunately the cheaper premises will probably not be notified to estate agents at all, but will depend on your ingenuity and energy to root them out. Any local organisation advising firms should be able to suggest ideas of whom to approach. Local authority planning departments can sometimes help, as they know what planning applications have been put in recently. In the countryside, the Country Landowners' Association and National Farmers' Union could know of something or put a note in their local newsletter about your problem. It may also be worth approaching agents for the local landed estates about redundant buildings that they may want to rent out.

When you do find your workshop you must tell the Health and Safety Executive (see the phone book) that you plan to use it. You should also tell the Fire Prevention Officer at the local Fire Brigade. Officials from both departments will come out to your proposed premises to give advice before you sign up. That avoids you finding out about the problems later, when it may be more costly to deal with them.

It is essential to think carefully about your present and future requirements of the building before making any commitment. Production, planning permission and building specialists are on hand from advisory agencies to help you to explore every aspect before you sign up.

7.5 Planning permission

Using any building or land for industrial or commercial purposes requires planning permission. You can try to get away without it but the odds are that you will get into trouble with the authorities sooner or later. Customers might be less than sympathetic to find that you are unable to deliver because the council has a court order forbidding you to work at your present premises.

Never assume that because Fred used the building before you it must be all right for you to use it. Perhaps Fred moved out due to council pressure. Or, on the other hand, perhaps the building has established industrial use rights. Or Fred may have been in a different official class of user: as a woodworker he could use it quite legitimately, but, running a sandwich bar, you may not.

The idea of established use rights is that if a building has been used continuously (and that means what it says – no gaps) for a particular activity since before 1965, it is assumed to have planning permission for the activity. This is true even if planning permission has never been applied for. You will obviously not assume that to be so, but will check with the planning department. If they say there is no problem, get them to confirm it in writing: this is very important.

They might ask you to apply for an Existing Use Certificate. That is a formal confirmation of the use rights, but it may tie the use down very tightly to exactly what was done previously, which could possibly be different from what you want to do. In that case you would have to apply for 'change of use'. Since each of those applications will cost about £50 for government fees alone, it is best to get advice. If the planning officer seems keen to help rather than hinder, his advice might be all you need. In other cases it could be better to consult a chartered surveyor, architect or solicitor, or one of the small firms agencies. If you choose one of the latter be sure to ask for at least three examples of local planning situations in which the adviser has been involved. The competent ones will have no trouble in reeling off a dozen or more. Those remarks also apply to a conventional planning application.

Six to eight weeks after the application the decision will be notified to you. If it is passed it will fall into one or more of these categories:

- *Full planning consent.* The building and land can be used by anyone forever for the activities specified in the consent document.

- *Temporary planning consent*. Can be used by anyone for the specified activities, but there will be a time limit, usually between one and five years. On expiry you can apply again.
- *Personal planning consent*. Only you may use the building and land. Anyone else wanting to take over the place from you will have to apply for a fresh planning consent.

Where a particularly sensitive site is concerned – say, in a residential area or a place of character and beauty – permission may be granted on both a personal and a temporary basis. This can also apply where the activity is one with, from the planners' point of view, a suspicious history. Motor vehicle repair is a good example. Mechanical repairers sometimes leave a mounting pile of old engine blocks and back axles lying around outside, and bodywork repairers have been known to assemble a growing heap of discarded panels and damaged body-shells. Giving temporary consent is a way of keeping you on your toes: any misbehaviour could be punished by refusal of your next application for renewal. If you have been a nuisance yet have heard no complaints it would be dangerous to assume that no one has complained to the council.

Both personal and temporary consent can present other difficulties. Financiers will find it hard to agree to lend money over a five-year period to a firm that has the right to use its premises for only two years. Likewise, you could question the wisdom of taking on such a commitment yourself. Similarly, if you have only personal consent for the use of a building you will want to keep to a minimum any investment in putting it in order. Perhaps the landlord will put it right for an increased rent? Spending thousands on rehabilitation out of your own pocket would make sense only if you were sure you would use it profitably for many years to come or that you could sell it on with continuing rights of use.

Even if a councillor or planning officer says that planning permission will be just a formality, do not assume it to be true. Many people who have gone ahead on a friendly nod and a wink are a lot poorer as a result.

In addition to the three broad categories laid down there will be detailed conditions attached to the consent. Almost always there are limits on the type of work that may be done, and on the hours of operation. There may be requirements to improve the access in the interests of road safety, to increase the car parking and manoeuvring area, to carry out planting or landscaping, and not to store anything out of doors. They should be taken seriously, but if any would cause you a great problem talk it over with the planning officer. He might be able to arrange for it to be varied, or you might have to appeal to the Secretary of State – see sections 7.7 and 7.8.

127

7.6 Applying for planning permission

There are forms to fill in, of course, but your approach to the planners should start long before you set pen to paper. Officially it is enough to fill in the forms, attach plans and a cheque and send them to your borough or district council. They would then be laid before the planning committee and the decision would come back six to eight weeks after the application went in. Unfortunately the whole system is run by human beings, so you must be very sure of success to do the officially required minimum and leave it at that. The planning officers (permanent, full-time officials) and the councillors (elected members of the council) are very busy people and are as capable as anyone of getting the wrong end of the stick. They are also subject to pressure from events – perhaps the chap they gave planning permission to six months ago has now created an eyesore – and from people like the local busybody who is getting up a petition against your plans. To stop those influences from working against you it is essential to influence the system in your favour. To do this it is best to start with a picture of how the system works.

When your completed form arrives at the planning office it is checked to see that it is filled in correctly and that you have sent in a cheque for the right amount. At the same time the official cannot avoid deciding whether or not he likes the proposal. Copies are sent to water, gas, electricity and roads authorities for their comments – you might plan to build right on top of a high-pressure gas main, or cause extra traffic to cross the road next to a lethal bend – and to the town or parish council for the comments of the body elected to represent the neighbouring community. Thus all sorts of people get to hear about it and, rightly, get the chance to protest before your application is considered officially by the planning committee.

In this situation the main enemy of common sense is ignorance of your real intentions. The forms you fill in give little enough information, so you need to spread more knowledge in the right quarters of what you are really up to. Invite the planning officer to view the site, describe your activities, explain how small and quiet your machines are, tell him you do not plan to run a fleet of lorries, and so on. In the nature of his work he is bound to be more aware of the small number of firms that cause nuisance than the large proportion that do not: make it clear which group you belong to. He might give advice on the best wording to use to describe your activity. Many small businessmen see officials as tiny-minded and obstructive. That is not always the case, and even if it is your view, remember that an official working for you is a lot better than one working the other way.

Next, invite the town or parish council to visit the site to prepare themselves for the application they will shortly receive. Ask the local councillor representing the area concerned to attend, too. Call personally on the people most likely to be affected, near neighbours especially, to explain yourself. Only then are you ready to fill in the forms. With them should go a letter that sums up briefly the sort of operation you plan to run. Then get every organisation you can think of to write in support of your application to the council – trade association, chamber of commerce, small firms' club, small business agency, and so forth. Then, and only then, can you be sure that you have done everything to ensure a fair hearing of your application. Planning committee meetings are public, so you may attend and listen, but not join in.

7.7 If you don't get the answer you wanted

The planning committee might give you permission with unacceptable conditions, or refuse an Existing Use Certificate, or even turn you down flat. Do not despair. First stop is the planning officer to find out exactly why, and to get advice on how to get the answer you want. Officials sometimes disagree with the decisions of their committees and can be very helpful in such circumstances. The best course may be to re-apply using a different form of wording to overcome any misunderstanding that you may unintentionally have brought about. Under those conditions your covering letter would explain the changes you have made and why.

Alternatively, or after a second application has failed, you can appeal to the Department of the Environment against the council's decision. Once an appeal has failed there is effectively no higher appeal. In theory you could go to the High Court, but that is very costly indeed. Hence the emphasis on re-applying rather than going straight to appeal.

7.8 Planning appeals

There are two forms of appeal. The public hearing is expensive – £1000 might cover a straightforward one – because you need to be professionally represented. The other sort is by written submissions. Either way, you must appeal within six months of the date of refusal, or have special permission for delay.

Most appeals involving small firms are written, so that method will be described. The form on which refusal is notified tells you the address to write to for the appeal forms. You fill them in and return them. A copy of your comments is sent to the council who reply with their views, a copy of which is sent to you. An inspector visits the site by appointment to let you and the council see that he carries out a proper inspection. He may ask questions for you to answer, but neither side is there to argue with the other or with him. Some inspectors carry their professional detachment so far as to decline a friendly offer to hold the end of the tape while they measure up. It normally takes the inspector between two and twelve months to get round to your appeal, and another month or two to give his decision. Once again the best course is not to do the whole thing unaided. You probably need advice from a chartered surveyor, architect or solicitor. Shop around to see what their record of success is in appeals, and to get quotes for the work. It is a specialised area and a lot may hang on the outcome, so professional help is advisable.

7.9 Leases

For all sorts of reasons, however straightforward a lease may seem, it should never be signed without the benefit of legal advice. Renting a building involves taking on a number of liabilities which are unavoidable, and others that you might be able to get out of. The ones you usually have to put up with include paying the landlord's legal costs as well as your own, and paying the landlord's insurance premium on the building itself. You are free, of course, to arrange your own insurance on your own things inside the building. It may be worth checking with your broker that the insurance premium you are being asked to pay the landlord is reasonable. You may hear the term 'full repairing and insuring' or FRI lease. That means that you are responsible for all insurances and repairs to the building. Fair enough, provided you do not find that it means you are expected to put things right that were already wrong before you moved in.

The way to protect yourself against this possibility is to get advice from a solicitor or chartered surveyor. He might suggest that the building should be carefully inspected and its existing condition photographed, and a schedule of condition agreed with the landlord. That would establish a benchmark for measuring what is your responsibility and what is not. Another good reason for taking advice is that the professionals have seen the problems before, and will protect you from future difficulty. What happens, for instance, if the roof gets wood-worm during your stay? Or if the existing, pleasant, landlord sells out to a really nasty successor? Often that can be more important even than the wording of documents, so it might be worth trying to find out your landlord's plans for the future.

7.10 Rates

Rates are charged on business premises by local authorities and water authorities in the same way as for houses. They can be a lot higher than people expect and, to rub salt in the wound, firms get fewer services than householders. Councils are actually forbidden by law from collecting refuse from many business premises without making a separate charge. People sometimes appeal against a rating assessment out of annoyance. It is wise to take professional advice beforehand – you would not want to draw attention to a property that had been under-rated for years, and get the opposite result from the one you wanted. If you use a lot of water it is worth discussing with the water authority the benefits of having your supply metered.

At the time of writing (late 1988) change is in the air. When the Community Charge replaces domestic rates a separate, national business rate will probably be set. At about the same time rateable values of business premises will be reassessed. It is not yet certain how big a rise in costs this will mean, but the pundits agree that a rise of some sort is almost inevitable.

Management of Operations

8.1 Aims of this section

Although it may look straightforward at first glance, the whole process of providing a service or manufacturing a product can become so complex and confused that you get more and more harassed while getting further behind. Planning and control of your activity are therefore vitally important. Just as you negotiate when selling, you can do the same when buying. Moreover, when buying you can be caught out by unscrupulous people, or just by simple misunderstandings. This section aims to deal with all of these issues, as well as to suggest that, as a first step, it might be best to find a firm with spare capacity to do the work for you.

8.2 Planning your activity

It seems obvious to say that you need to think ahead and to plan, but so many people have gone into business and then found that they rented premises of the wrong size or shape, or that their equipment will not do what is expected of it, or that the time allowed for jobs is never enough, or that they keep running out of materials. If they are honest, they all agree that they could have foreseen and avoided such problems. Of course, there are always extenuating circumstances – we all like to save face and blame anything but our own foolishness.

How do you stop all this from happening to you? You can never avoid errors completely, but a little planning will save a lot of hassle, and make life smoother for you – and for your customers. Also, try to learn from experience: know what went wrong, and take it into account next time. To be able to do this, you need records of what happened.

8.3 Control of your operation

To look in detail at the control methods that you can use, we might start with the individual job. Each should have its own job card which follows it through the production process. Each job card records:

- Job reference number and description

- Customer's reference number for the job, and order number
- References to drawings, catalogues etc
- Route to be followed through the production process
- Completion date estimated for each stage of production
- Materials needed
- Special tooling needed
- Time estimated for in each department or in each process
- Name of each operative working on this job
- Packing instructions.

This sets up the main headings which enable your aspirations for the job to be laid down. To turn the planning document into one that can achieve control, a box needs to be set against each heading in which *actual* performance is recorded. Regular and frequent inspection of job cards enables you to see which jobs and processes are falling behind schedule, so that some sort of action can be taken.

In addition, such a system offers other benefits. At the end of the week the hours recorded by each employee can be totalled to show the productive hours that he has apparently put in. If the hours shown add up to more than he has been present for, either you are getting more out of him than any boss has a right to expect, or something needs investigating. Likewise for the employee who records far fewer hours than you pay him for. If this is your only control over the efficiency of the way you use staff, they will quickly learn to adjust the records so as to make you happy. Nevertheless, though crude, this can be a useful pointer to inefficiencies. Another advantage of a system like this is that you learn where your estimating method is going wrong, by comparing estimate with reality. Furthermore, you spot bottlenecks before they occur; job cards that show a requirement for more than you can get out of a department or a machine quickly highlight the need to acquire more capacity, subcontract some work or revise delivery dates.

In addition to controls over individual jobs, you will need to oversee production as a whole. The form of those controls depends largely on the kind of business you are in. Common to all businesses is the need to understand:

- Extent of forward commitments
- Spare capacity in each process or at each machine
- Scheduling of the next work to be done
- Holiday schedules
- Machinery maintenance timetables
- Use of capacity against the level budgeted for
- Scrap and rework rates.

If your business undertakes 'specials', additional forms of control will include:

- Progress of each job against deadlines
- Availability of special materials needed
- Progress on producing quotations
- Proportion of quotations that turn into orders.

On the other hand, if you make items that are kept in stock, your priorities will be different. You will focus on:

- 'Free' stock levels of finished goods (ie total stock, less orders received but not yet delivered)
- Materials stocks and reorder lead times
- Making economic batches, yet not over-stocking
- Relating production capacity and stock levels to sales forecasts.

As well as looking at the capacity of your equipment, you should look at that of your people. Do they need to master new skills to handle the work that you expect to be getting? Do they have the tools and working conditions that they need? Does everything they need have a sensible place? Is it in that place? What will you do if a key person retires or leaves for another reason? Above all, do *you* make it easy or hard for them to do their jobs well?

Talk about control systems is all very well, but thought also needs to be given to the way in which information is presented. All those chalkboards, whiteboards, charts and graphs in offices are not there to impress visitors; they are doing a job of work. Not all of the information in your firm should be on public display, but it certainly should be readily available to you at a glance in summary form. Then you stand a chance of running the firm rather than having it run you.

People walking into small firms' premises are too often confronted by muddle and mess. When materials and equipment are needed they cannot be found, causing a loss of valuable time. Spare parts and components get lost and damaged, raising costs still further. As such a firm grows, it sometimes takes on expensive space, rather than sort out the confusion. Yet the simple act of clearing up often releases space to enable expansion to take place much more cheaply.

On the other hand, there are the blessed few firms whose premises are spick and span with everything in its allotted place. The atmosphere of smooth, business-like activity tells you everything you need to know about its management. Compare these two sorts of place, from the points of view of good-quality staff, customers and bank managers. Which is more likely to get and keep the best people? Which will give a customer the better impression? Where does the bank manager feel that he ought to invest his shareholders' money? Neither set-up came about by some mysterious process unknown to mortal man, but each was *directly caused* by its manager's attitudes, ideas and methods.

The effect of your behaviour on the way that your staff perform is discussed in section 10. For the present it is enough to say that your example and leadership are most important. Even the best manager does not get production from his staff 100 per cent of the time, however. Earlier discussion of the one-man firm suggested that when you were the sole employee, you would probably manage to produce for 25 hours out of the 60 or so you worked in total. This is about a 40 per cent efficiency. Since your staff will not have the same range of non-productive activity to perform as you do, their efficiency ought to be at or around 70 per cent to 75 per cent. In other words, if you are paying for 40 hours' work, you can realistically expect it to yield about 30 hours' production. To get it to that level and to hold it there demands that you constantly ask of your staff that they set a brisk place. In agriculture they say that the best fertiliser is the farmer's boot; frequent and detailed checks by the boss are what ensure the best harvest. The same goes for production areas.

Staff are the scarcest and most costly item in many small firms. It therefore makes sense to keep them working even when demand falls. In some markets sometimes prices have to be cut. If your business is like this, it is worth talking to a production specialist with a costing background, or an accountant with production experience, about the various methods of costing. Some of them might throw up an opportunity for an occasional tactical price cut to keep the factory employed. Expert advice is essential, for this is a risky field.

In considering the way that your people use their time, do not avoid looking at all aspects. Your effect on them has been mentioned, but you might also consider the rules that you lay down for:

- Hours of work. Could 8 to 5 be extended to 8 to 5.30?
- *Tea-breaks*. Do people need to leave their work stations to have a drink? In some activities it is desirable that they do, but could your people take the drink at their work?
- *Lunch-breaks*. Is a whole hour necessary, or desirable?
- *Time-keeping*. A 10-minute tea-break can easily drift into a 20- or 30-minute period once washing, popping out for some cigarettes, and discussing last night's TV have been got through.
- *Punctuality*. A 7.30 start should mean exactly that, not a 7.30 arrival and a start at 7.45; a 5 o'clock finish does not mean breaking off at quarter-to to start getting ready for the off.

If that sounds penny-pinching, think of the effect of letting things drift. Just by banishing tea-breaks and ensuring a punctual start and finish, you could employ one person less in every six or seven. That is not greed on your part, for it means greater efficiency for your firm which will enable it to beat off less disciplined competitors. In turn that implies more job security for your staff, which they might need reminding of.

A final few words on control, to do with keeping control of your stock. Remember the Forces' maxim, that nothing moves without a piece of paper: relying on memory and honesty are simply not enough.

8.4 Safety

Keep the working area clean and clear of obstructions and hazards; call in an outsider for a safety inspection, and shock yourself with the number of dangers that there are, and put things right straightaway. After all, you have no immunity against injury, and if you are off for a month, or lose an eye, or three fingers, who will run the business and keep your family? Even if you are insured, your income will be very low. And be careful when lifting: do not try proving to yourself, or to anyone else, how tough you are. Ask anyone with a hernia or slipped disc what it is like to live with. Display the statutory notices and read them (heavy going they may be, but they could save your life), and have some way of raising the alarm if you get hurt. Again, it is so obvious it should not need saying, but thousands every year ignore it and pay the price: observe the safety rules, work at a safe pace, use machine guards, never take risks, and wear the right protective gear.

You are legally obliged by the Health and Safety at Work Act to work safely and to ensure that your staff do the same, as well as to keep a record of any unsafe incidents. Consult the Factory Inspector – he is in the phone book under 'Health and Safety Executive'.

8.5 Purchasing

This is the mirror-image of selling, and you will be fascinated to observe the techniques of persuasion that are used by the salesmen who call on you. As well as educating you in salesmanship, they could of course rob you, so a healthy dash of scepticism is needed in dealing with them. Salesmen are eager to please, and without meaning to mislead can let you think that their product will do things that it cannot. Once more it seems so obvious, but so many people starting businesses buy pigs in pokes, and especially equipment they expect will do a particular job without really checking. Always, without exception, shop around. Usually the only reason for the seller to push for a fast decision is precisely to stop you from finding out just how common and cheap is his allegedly unique and expensive product. So get alternative quotes.

Get salesmen to criticise their competitors' products: like all of us, they are usually better at pointing out the shortcomings of others than of themselves. Then let them answer the criticisms of their own product. This applies ten times over if you are not familiar with the process, materials or technology involved. Here, you need specialist help before making any commitment, perhaps from one of the agencies listed in section 12. Do not let yourself be pushed into buying more than you need or can afford. Any salesman is happier with half a loaf than no bread, and if you stand firm he will either miraculously find a way of sending you a smaller order than the previously sacred minimum – as a special personal favour, of course – or fix up something with another customer so that you can buy a little from him. If you have thought out properly in advance what you need the equipment or material to do, and have specified this to the salesman, he can tell you whether or not his wares meet your requirements. He will then be lucky if he can shift you from what is best for you to what is best for him – and remember, however plausible and fair-minded he may seem, that is exactly what he is paid for. In front of him, write down and date a note of the points that are important to you, and the promises he makes, and read them back to him. He should then be very careful what he says, and you will get only reliable information. (If you ever sell to a really professional buyer, the odds are that his secretary will be sitting in the corner behind you. It is no accident that she does not type while you are there – she is taking shorthand notes of everything you say.) And don't forget that the law of contract applies to verbal agreements, so do not say that you will buy without really meaning it, and never, ever, give a salesman an order to make him go away. Just tell him to go away – it is quicker and certainly cheaper.

8.6 Negotiating when buying

As a small business you may feel you have no buying power at all. Possibly that is true, but often it is not. Whatever your position, you can usually improve it. If they want you to order by phone, try to get them to send a salesman. If he makes the visit, he will be keener to justify it by getting an order and opening a new account, so he may give away a discount or let you have a promotional offer that you do not really qualify for. You need to build up your case: he is a nice chap, his products are good, but his competitor is making a powerful pitch; and his goods are not exactly what you want ... Leave it in the air, and let him try to think of how to persuade you. Keep on coming back with objections (and a smile) and keep showing interest, and sooner or later he will get round to thinking about reducing the price or increasing the value in some other way. How nice of him, that offer does really make the decision a lot easier, but you cannot agree to the conditions attached to it. Finally, he gives in and you buy what you intended to buy all along but on much better terms.

If the firm deals from a trade counter you will find it difficult to use these tactics on the warehousemen behind the counter. They are just there to fetch and carry, and the printed price-list is law as far as they are concerned. That is exactly the company's game – to make it look as if you are dealing with a brute machine rather than human beings open to persuasion. So refuse to play the game, but ask to see the manager about opening a new trade account. When you get face to face with him, or with the rep they may send out to see if you are a genuine business, you can try negotiating discounts and credit exactly as suggested above. The more impersonal the contact, the more you are forced to accept their terms, so try to make it personal. If he is a constant supplier, keep the relationship going – send him a Christmas card at least, and don't abuse the credit terms too much. If you cannot pay this month, let him know that it will help your cash flow greatly if he would allow you a couple of weeks' extra credit. Do not wait until you appear on his 'Stop' list.

8.7 Quality control

Even if it means delivery will be late, check quality before your product leaves your workshop. A few hours' lateness gets you less of a bad reputation than a delivery of faulty goods made on time. Consignments of goods delivered to you should be checked for completeness, freedom from damage, and quality, as soon as they are received. Any shortcomings or shortage should be notified by phone and confirmed by letter immediately. If you leave it until later, it may be too late for your claim to be verified as the carrier holds his 'proof of delivery' documents for only a short time. You can then find yourself forced to pay for something you did not receive. If you let anyone take back goods that are damaged or faulty, do get him to sign for them, and to print his name. Otherwise some slip-up or change of staff by the supplier (and they do happen all the time) could mean you can't prove that you no longer have the goods, so you still have to pay.

You may hear mention of BS 5750. That is a fairly new British Standard covering quality control, and major buyers of engineering goods are increasingly insisting that their suppliers should observe it. Details can be had from small firms agencies and from the British Standards Institution.

8.8 Product design

In many companies there is a constant tug-of-war between the selling side, who would love to have products personalised for each customer, and the production people, who can see the benefits of standardised manufacturing. In the very small firm this struggle goes on in the head of the owner, who can feel completely bemused by the choices before him. In the end he will recognise that the customers' needs come first, but no chance should be lost to standardise where possible. The benefits are obvious: simplicity, economy, lower stocks, less design time, and so on. Even where quite different end products are being made, it might be possible to standardise some components or sub-assemblies – but only within the limits of customer acceptability. It is worth checking with customers what they will accept: products are often wildly over-specified because the engineer thought that this was what was needed, whereas the customer would have been delighted with something less substantial or complex.

Although this section is to do with production matters, a few words should be said about the marketing aspect of design. The textbooks are full of classic stories about minor changes to specification, or just to appearance, that transformed the appeal of a product. It can work for your products, too. But the very best design-led marketing successes usually involve much more. They show that designers who address basic marketing principles are the big winners. Instead of titivating a product's cosmetic appeal they go right to the root of the customer's real needs. They deliver better *value*, which does not just mean cutting prices (see section 2.9).

Bookkeeping, Financial Housekeeping, VAT and Tax

9.1 Aims of this section

This section highlights some points on keeping simple but clear records and tries to demystify the dreaded VAT. It does not contain an attempt to train you in bookkeeping: it takes the view that as little time as possible should be spent on this chore consistent with accuracy, keeping within the law, and providing information for you to know where the business is going.

9.2 Bookkeeping

In the excitement of starting a business, many people forget the importance of the records that the State and others will expect them to keep. It is easy to get into trouble, and then try to rescue yourself, but better to set up a good administrative system from the start and operate it properly. So you will do yourself a considerable favour by getting this under way well in advance of actually starting to make and to sell. How to do it? If you try to do it yourself the traditional 'double entry' way, you may need a lot of training. It is unwise to set up your own system, however simple your business might be at first. Unfortunately, a do-it-yourself set of books has a nasty habit of being unable to cope with unforeseen complications. The professional productions take them into account. The sensible alternative is to use one of the simplified systems like Safeguard or Kalamazoo. They are not hard to master and the people who make them will always help out if you get stuck. Clear with your accountant which system you plan to use, and make sure that simpler records for you do not mean more work for him (and thus higher fees for you to pay). Or you could use one of the bookkeeping services that are often run from a person's home. That is not recommended as first choice – you should run your own accounts and know what is going on financially in the firm.

Absolutely the way not to do it is to do no bookkeeping until you have accumulated a carrier bag full of cheque-book stubs, bank statements, invoices, and so on, and then dump the lot on your accountant. He will sort it out for you, but at a price that will make your hair curl. To avoid this, systems can be developed of varying complexity. The simplest of all is one based on the four drawers of your desk, or four files or, indeed, four old shoeboxes. Two drawers are used for invoices that are unpaid – one for purchases, one for sales. When invoices are paid, they move across to the other two drawers. The point is that no invoices go astray, and by adding up the contents of the 'unpaid' drawers you see exactly what you owe and are owed. Your cheque book and paying-in book complete the picture by enabling you to work out how much is in the bank. The very simplest type of business can probably manage on this, but only if it never needs to get quick information on profits.

The next stage up is the simplified system already referred to. Thereafter, you might move up to a more sophisticated 'one-entry' system, where putting in one figure can complete more than one essential record. Then to a full double-entry system designed in conjunction with your accountant. Or even, perhaps, to a computerised system. If and when you do use a micro-computer for bookkeeping, take proper advice and remember that the system must be approved by Customs and Excise for VAT calculations before you install it. Try to avoid the temptation to go for anything less than a fully proven business system.

All bookkeeping needs to be done promptly – at least weekly, preferably daily. Receipts must be got and kept for every purchase, and bank statements should be carefully checked against cheque and paying-in books. And they have to be kept for years, to satisfy the tax authorities.

9.3 Bank accounts

A very small sole trader or partnership can easily get business transactions mixed up with personal money. The simplest way of operating to avoid this is to have two bank accounts, each with its own cheque book. One is your personal account, or joint account with your spouse, out of which you pay all the personal and home bills, and draw your pocket money. The other, the business or Number Two account, is kept to the business only. In addition to paying the business creditors and receiving the business income, it pays a wage (known to accountants as 'drawings') to your personal, or Number One, account. There is nothing to say you have to keep business and personal accounts at the same bank, although bank managers like to have both under their control.

9.4 Value Added Tax – VAT – in outline

This tax had a really bad press when it was introduced. One reason was that it was new and different, and any new tax is worth a good moan.

Another was that HM Customs and Excise were chosen to administer it, bringing with them in some cases the attitudes and methods that so effectively enable them to sniff out illegal drugs buried in the depths of 50,000-ton ships. Since the early days there have been none of the headlines about persecution of little old ladies running sweet shops and it has settled down to being just another routine chore. At the same time, you should not forget that in extreme cases HM Customs has the right to confiscate most of your records for investigation, and thus practically to close you down, so they should be treated with respect. Look up Customs and Excise in the phone book and ask for their free leaflets and any advice on special VAT situations which may arise with your firm. A simplified explanation of the principles follows.

Products you sell can be taxed either at standard rate (15 per cent at the time of writing), or at zero rate (strictly speaking, 0 per cent, so not taxed at present but the mechanism is there if the government feels like imposing it), or exempt altogether. Let us say that you are registered for VAT and sell 10 widgets, which are standard-rated, at £10 each to XZ Ltd, and your invoice says: '10 Widgets at £10 = £100 + VAT = £115 payable'. The £15 tax is called an 'output', the name in VAT jargon for the tax on the goods you sell. Now for – you guessed it – 'inputs'. That is the tax on your purchases. For the sake of the illustration, you buy in unfinished blanks for widgets from Smith Stampings, and their invoice says '10 Widget blanks at £1 = £10 + £1.50 VAT = £11.50 payable'. That £1.50 is of course your 'input', the VAT on your purchase. So far, so good. At the end of the quarter, you send in a return to HM Customs and Excise, showing your total inputs and your total outputs. If you have charged out (say) £1000 of output tax and have been invoiced for £800 of input tax, you send a cheque for the £200 difference. On the other hand, if you invoice for only £800 of output tax and are charged for £1000 of tax on inputs, HM Customs and Excise will send you a cheque for £200.

In principle, it really is that simple, but you should remember that only VAT-registered bodies are allowed to show VAT on an invoice. That does not deter some tricksters who charge VAT even though unregistered. The resulting loss is carried by the poor mug who paid out the alleged VAT unless he can recover it through the courts.

9.5 Registering for VAT

You are not compelled to register for VAT if you are working in a very small way. Equally, you can de-register if your sales fall below the limits. At the time of writing (tax year 1988/89) the limit for compulsory registration is a turnover of £22,100 in a year, or £7,500 in any one quarter: it is raised from time to time in the Budget to allow for inflation.

While you do not have to register in your early days if you are very small, it can be worth doing. You are allowed to under a system called 'Voluntary Registration'. The main snag is that you must remain registered for at least two years. The motive for doing so is if you pay out a lot of VAT on equipment or stock that you buy before you have built up sales to the limit where you must register. It enables you to claim back the VAT on those early purchases as an input. Bear in mind that VAT on cars cannot be reclaimed, but vans are different. Before setting up, consult Customs and Excise and your accountant about when would be best to register.

Another aspect of that decision is how it affects your prices. If you sell to the public, it makes no odds whether your price is £115, or £100 + £15 VAT = £115. On the other hand, if you sell to businesses registered for VAT, and most are, there is a lot of difference. To a business customer an invoice for £100 + £15 VAT means that the goods cost £100: the £15 is merely part of a tax-collecting exercise, to be offset by his inputs at the end of the quarter.

9.6 Income tax and corporation tax

The Inland Revenue Inspectors of Taxes publish an excellent free leaflet called 'Starting in Business' (IR28). It outlines your position so well that there is no point in repeating it all here. It even includes Form 41G on which to notify your local Inspector of Taxes that you are starting a business.

9.7 National Insurance

Although it started off more or less as a State insurance arangement, NI has now become virtually another income tax. As a self-employed person (active partner, or sole trader) you have to pay Class 2 contributions weekly which are at a straightforward flat rate. On top of that you pay a Class 4 contribution which is earnings-related on profits (or salary and fees instead or as well if you are a director) between certain limts. The Department of Social Security collect Class 2s by direct debit on your bank account or by the old-fashioned stamps that you stick on to a contribution card. Direct debit is the better way to do it, as people who choose to stamp cards so often fall behind – and once behind it is difficult to catch up. The Class 4 contribution is collected by the Inland Revenue. Leaflets giving details are listed in IR28 (see section 9.6 above) and all are free. More information appears in sections 5.3 and 5.5 of this book.

9.8 Tax reliefs

Most of the expenditure on items connected with business are allowable for tax relief. There may be some that you do not automatically think of, and again your accountant's advice is vital before you start in business or even start buying things for the firm. If you work from home you may be tempted to claim tax relief on part of the household expenses and it might be granted, but when you sell the house the Inland Revenue might, in return, claim capital gains tax on part of the proceeds (homes are normally exempt from CGT). Again, check with your accountant. A basic understanding of tax is important to a businessman but it is such a complex field that professional advice is essential before decisions are taken.

When you start in business on your own you may be able to claim back some of the tax you have paid in previous years. This does not apply if you trade as a limited company, but only if you are self-employed as a sole trader or partner. It all revolves around the idea of 'tax losses'. A tax loss need not be a real loss – indeed, highly profitable companies try to acquire them all the time. To take an example:

In the same tax year

Net profit before tax	£5,000
Tax allowance	£15,000
Tax loss	£10,000

The £10,000 'loss' can be claimed against earlier taxed income. It can be seen that the company used as an example was in fact profitable – it made £5,000 – but it chose to invest some of its cash (and/or some loan – we are not told) in new equipment. In return, the tax man will chip in with an offer to let the firm carry forward that £10,000 tax allowance into future years, or to repay tax paid on £10,000-worth of income in earlier years. This concession extends over the first four years of the new firm's life, and allows the back claim to refer to as much as the total of all the tax paid in the three years before setting up. If your firm might want to take advantage of this arrangement, careful timing of your formal start is advisable, which needs the expert help of your accountant.

Tax allowances usually arise because the business has bought a capital asset against which the tax man permits a 'writing-down allowance' each year. On motor vehicles it is 25 per cent and on machines and equipment 20 per cent in 1988/89. Thus the business quoted above might have spent £50,000 on machinery within the last five years (20 per cent of £50,000 = £10,000 writing-down allowance). Allowances are also available against property, but at much lower rates.

Employing People

10.1 Aims of this section

Life would be simpler for many businessmen if they could do everything themselves and manage without staff. In some businesses it is possible to do just that, but problems come when you want to expand. Better organisation and more mechanisation may help up to a point, but if you have any growth ambitions at all you usually find that you become an employer before very long. This section aims to point out the main traps and to help you to avoid them.

10.2 The law: a big problem?

Most of the small business horror stories centre around employment law, ending on the refrain, 'you can't sack anyone these days'. Don't believe it. Certainly, you are not allowed to play ducks and drakes with employees' livelihoods in the way that our great-grandfathers could. But the reasonable, decent employer has very little to fear from the law. The biggest problem he has is in minimising and solving the problems that he causes his employees, finding good staff in the first place, and finding the time to spend with them to ensure that they stay. To help him, the Department of Employment publishes dozens of free leaflets describing his obligations and rights. They are available from Jobcentres.

10.3 Finding good people

The first job, as with any other management task, is to decide what you want done and how. In other words, define the job systematically, without any fixed ideas about who should do it. Think about what needs to be done now, of course, but also how it will evolve in the future. What special qualities are needed to do all this? You are now able to get a picture of the person; if a mature telephone manner is essential, a 17-year-old is unlikely to suit. If you might want them to work a microcomputer within a couple of years, many 60-year-olds might not have the flexibility to absorb the training. Equally, if the job is likely to change dramatically in three years' time, it could be worth taking on

145

someone who is three years from retirement and recruit new people for the new job after two and a half years. Where and how do you find good people? In three main ways: putting the word out, advertising, or going to an employment agency. Each has its benefits and drawbacks. The author's preference – though it does not suit everyone – is for the ads that you place yourself. They cost money whether or not you find someone (agencies charge only for people recruited) but you control exactly what the ad says and how you are described; not all agency staff are so careful. Application forms are a must, to check on candidates' writing ability and presentation, to give you a written and signed record of the applicant's past achievements and to protect you from charges of discrimination. One day you might be asked to prove that you selected a candidate on the basis of qualifications for the job, and that sex, colour and religious beliefs, did not come into it.

10.4 The interview

Having received the completed application forms you are now ready to call people for interview. Although time will be short, you should try to hold more than one interview, and to have someone else present whose views you respect. Typically (depending on the job) you might ask seven people to first interviews and shortlist three for your final choice. Make allowances for interview nerves, try to put candidates at ease, but do not give more than an outline sketch of the job itself until after you have drawn out of the candidate what he or she is looking for, is good at, is bad at, and wants to avoid in a new job. Take up references from previous employers if candidates give their permission: the only objection should be to approaching the current employer before a job offer has been made and accepted. When taking up references, do it by telephone and get exact dates as far as possible. Why? There may be something that the employee wants to hide – and that, by definition, is what you want to know about. It is worth mentioning here that your employee nowadays has legal immunity from telling the truth about old criminal convictions, and you cannot fire him if you find out about it later. So if that is important to you, your checking needs to be very thorough before any job offer is made.

10.5 References

As discussed in section 10.4, a satisfactory reference from the current or last employer should be obtained. It should agree on the main facts and the exact period of employment, but the rest should be taken with caution. Spite, self-justification, rationalisation, all can play a part in how a reference is phrased. An unwise employer will give a good reference to an employee whom he wants to see the back of. Unwise, because you could claim damages if you lost as a result. For example, someone who had been suspected of fiddling is given a reference for exemplary honesty. Let us say that there was not enough evidence to prosecute, but some was building up. He then joins you, and six months later you find that he has helped himself to £2000. You would probably have a case against the former employer. For just that sort of reason, you in your turn would be wise not to give references. Of course, you want to help former employees, so you do not refuse a reference outright – that looks like a condemnation in itself – but you send a standard letter which confirms that Mr Smith worked for you from June 1986 to February 1988 and was employed as a driver, rising to warehouse supervisor, but going on to say that it is your company's practice never to comment on any employee's performance or reasons for leaving.

10.6 The job offer and its acceptance

The offer should be made in a letter, with written acceptance by the successful candidate. Do not turn down the unsuccessful candidates until you have written confirmation that the job has been accepted. Incidentally, if an applicant accepts a job offer and then does not start, causing you the trouble of readvertising, he could be liable to pay the costs (but you could have trouble getting them from him). When he joins, tell the local Income Tax office, who will give you the necessary forms and tax tables. If he is under 18, then notify the local Careers Office.

10.7 Getting who you want, and making sure they stay

Nothing is forever, so always know what you will do if a key employee gives a week's notice just as you are off on three weeks' holiday. Blame yourself if you are unprepared. You could not have blamed him if he had died, yet the effect is the same. Equally, you should never get into the position where a key part of your business is out of your control and is understood by only one of your employees. If he or she is the only one who knows the way round parts of the business, not only can you not afford to lose that person but you are also open to being defrauded. Remember, too, that it is easy to make staff disgruntled. Treat them badly, and you can be sure that any suffering that they experience will rebound tenfold on you. If you manage your people well, you do yourself, as well as them, a favour. The right way to treat employees is the way you would expect to be treated yourself: openly, honestly, equally with other employees, being told unpleasant news straightfor-wardly, being expected to contribute fully, and having effort recognised. Your employees will not have the grievances there are in so many larger firms: dealing with frightened superiors who dare not give decisions, seeing the bosses arriving at 9 o'clock (with no clocking-on) when they have clocked on at 7.30 am, seeing white-collar staff getting separate (and better) dining arrangements, and so on. Your staff will know that you work harder and longer than they do, in the same conditions, and that is what earns you the respect that few managers ever command in larger firms. You might not be able to pay them as much as a bigger firm – but you might have to. It is worth not being flamboyant in the type of car you get. An old Aston-Martin, or a new Ford, may not be over-doing things, but you tempt your employees to think how much they have contributed to a new Aston-Martin, Maserati or Porsche.

While you will want your employees to share in the success that they have helped to create, beware of bonus schemes. The annual Christmas bonus rapidly becomes thought of as a natural entitlement and loses motivating power, and bonuses based on output can cause more ill-feeling than almost anything else. Probably the best – or least bad – scheme is one based on value added. Your best bet is to seek specialist advice on its design and installation. Pension schemes and medical insurance schemes are worth looking at. Pensions are almost esssential for good staff, and it should be a scheme which makes it easy for staff to transfer their accumulated rights into it on joining, and out of it on leaving.

Although people may be employed for 40 hours a week, they cannot work effectively for all of that time. Most firms think that they do well to get 30 hours' production from a week's work, and many get far less. See sections 3.4 and 8.3.

10.8 Contracts of employment

You are obliged by law to give a 'written statement' of the terms of the contract of employment within 13 weeks of the employee joining you. It applies only to employees working at least 16 hours a week. As you will know from section 6 on law, the contract exists even if it is not written down. To keep the relationship with your employee clear and above board, the written statement should be given at the earliest stage of the employment – say, during the first week. The written statement has by law to contain the particulars listed below. But you should not try to write your own. It is full of pitfalls and needs advice from someone experienced in the field. The usual advisory agencies can help, as could a lecturer in industrial relations from your local college, polytechnic or university. Your solicitor is technically capable of writing it, but may slip into legalese in its wording.

The employee's reaction to a document not written in plain language may be to run straight to his trade union for advice and protection – not quite what you wanted to achieve.

The written statement of the terms of employment should show:

- Names of the employer and employee
- When the employment began
- When the period of *continuous* employment began; for example, staff working for a firm that you took over would have this period operating from when they started work for the firm, not from the take-over
- The date of expiry, if employment is for a fixed term
- Job title
- How pay is calculated, the pay rate and the pay period (hourly, weekly, monthly)
- Normal working hours and overtime requirements
- Holiday entitlements, holiday pay calculation, public holidays
- Sickness and injury absence rules
- Sick pay calculations
- Pension scheme details, if any, and whether or not the employment is contracted out of the State scheme
- Length of notice required and given
- Disciplinary rules
- The person to whom the employee should apply if dissatisfied with a disciplinary ruling
- The person to whom the employee can take a grievance connected with work.

The last two items, disciplinary and grievance procedures, may be shown in separate documents to which employees have access –the usual place is the staff notice board. The same goes for the firm's health and safety policy (yes, you should have one of those too).

Each of these papers needs proper and careful design by a specialist. The list above is shown so that you can brief your adviser properly, and thus use less of his time, which will be costing somebody money.

Not only do they deserve specialist attention, but they should also be written with an individual business – your business – in mind. Again, the advisers can help. Indeed, the Rural Development Commission's Business Service and other development agencies have on their staff specialists who offer this service. As an alternative, a standard form can be bought from a commercial stationer, but this seems too impersonal for a firm that is trying to show its staff that they are valued. To the boss, the written statement may be an irritating routine matter, to be got out of the way as soon as possible. But to the staff it is an important document which confirms what the boss thinks of them, and speaking volumes about how he plans to treat them. And they have to be given it by the time they have been with you for three months – just about the time when the jobs that they did not get, or declined, might become free again. If the headhunter phones your new young star at home one evening, the last thing you want is for him to start talking seriously about a possible move. So do not encourage it by giving him the wrong sort of written statement.

10.9 Employment protection

In a company employing no more than 20, two years after the employee joins he or she qualifies for protection from dismissal without good reason. The two-year immunity does not apply if you employed more than 20 at any time during the two years, or if you dismiss on grounds of race or sex, or because the employee becomes pregnant, or has to do with trade union activity, or because the employee has not disclosed a 'spent' criminal conviction. The immunity is for one year for firms employing 21 or more. Other conditions worth knowing about are that the employee must have worked for two years for at least 16 hours per week, or five years for eight hours per week, to be protected. If you employ five people or fewer, a pregnant employee does not have the right to insist on reinstatement if it is not reasonably practicable for you to take her back following the birth. In larger firms she can insist, subject to certain conditions being met.

10.10 Industrial Tribunals

If an employee feels that he has been dismissed unfairly you could be hauled up before the well-known Industrial Tribunal, where the onus will be on you to prove that you did dismiss fairly. The employer is guilty unless he can prove himself innocent! But things are not as bad as they seem. Before all this happens, the employee will have put his case in writing – he has three months to do so after leaving your employment, or he loses his rights – and you will have put your side in return, with the help of your solicitor, of course. An officer from ACAS will then try to sort things out between you, and should succeed unless one of you is being really pig-headed. If the matter is settled at that stage, so be it. If not, the ACAS officer will report to the Tribunal and it will not look too good if you come out of that looking stubborn and inflexible. You and the ex-employee will give evidence, which is at least one day out of the office (plus solicitors' fees for a day) and the Tribunal will usually give its decision there and then. The awards can be several thousand pounds, so it is worth fighting if you have a good case. If your case is bad, bargain with the ex-employee through ACAS to try to get him to accept a cash payment in full and final settlement of his claim. ACAS will record it in such a way that his claim is withdrawn. If either side ignores the ACAS arbitrator's recommendation and insists on pushing ahead to a full Tribunal hearing he risks having costs awarded against him.

10.11 Fair dismissal

To dismiss fairly you have to prove you acted reasonably, given all the circumstances, and that the reason for dismissal was admissible. Admissible reasons are redundancy, misconduct, incapacity for the work, some other major reason why you could not keep the employee on (such as strong personality conflict), or if by keeping him on you would break the law. The way you handled it also affects the Tribunal's view of whether or not you acted 'reasonably' (see sections 10.12 and 10.13).

10.12 Disciplinary procedures

A rather forbidding title for a very necessary subject. You need to lay down these procedures and to stick to them in the interests of fairness, consistency, and being on the right side of the law. If someone misbehaves really badly you could sack him on the spot: in your disciplinary procedure you can list examples of behaviour which fall into this category. They might include drunkenness, horseplay, violence, theft, refusal to carry out lawful instructions, unjustified absence, wilful damage to company property, unauthorised removal of property from company premises, disobeying safety rules – and that is not a full list, and neither should yours attempt to be.

It should be made clear that it illustrates only the sort of offence involved, as there may be others which apply to your type of work. A printer, for instance, could reasonably sack on the spot someone who smoked in the paper store. As it happens, you would be ill-advised to sack instantly – far better to send the employee home, suspended on full pay (it is illegal not to pay him) while you cool off and get to the facts of the case. After all, the chap you catch putting a typewriter into the boot of his car may have been told by your foreman that it is OK to borrow it over the weekend to type the circulars for the church jumble sale. Of course, serious misconduct is one thing, and minor matters are another. A man who is repeatedly late with no good excuse can be even more of a problem than the one who takes two days 'sick' for a mid-week football match. Similarly, there are other minor offences that you cannot let slide. If things get so bad that you have to dismiss, you should have built up a case and recorded it in writing. The first instance should attract a verbal warning which is noted on his file. A written warning would be issued for the second, making it clear that a repetition could lead to dismissal. On the third offence he could be sacked, and the reasons put in writing with your solicitor's help. Of course you do not sack someone for three minor offences in five years. Perhaps you would put a time limit on the record and ignore them in this 'totting up' procedure if they were more than six months old.

10.13 Grievance procedure

So far we have looked at the trouble that misbehaving employees can cause you. But you, their boss, can be as big a problem to them, or more so, because they can rarely put you out of a job, while you have the power to do that to them. So fair dealing requires that they can question any unfair decision. The mirror-image of the disciplinary procedure is the grievance procedure. If the employee feels that you have dealt harshly or unfairly with him, he should have the right to complain formally. In large firms, these formal procedures can be very complex, involving unions, works councils, ACAS, and heaven knows who else. In very small companies the appeal is usually straight back to the boss. That can make it a bit ticklish: who does the chap think he is, questioning your instructions? In the hurly-burly it is easy to react instinctively, but in the interests of good management it is worth hearing him out. You will not be the first boss to be saved by one of the lads from doing something which would have unintended, unjust side-effects, or from asking the impossible, or from giving contradictory orders; so listen. Most complaints stop there and are sorted out on the spot. If, however, your considered view is that a collision is inevitable in the best interests of the business it would be as well to hold a formal grievance meeting at which notes would be taken of both sides' views. If things ever escalated you would thank your lucky stars that evidence of such a meeting was available for your solicitor to build into your case.

If at all possible, have two tiers in your grievance procedure, the foreman being the first, with you as the final arbiter. At least in the early days of your firm that is unlikely to be possible, but you can introduce it as you grow.

10.14 Redundancy

If work falls off you can sack people by this route quite straightforwardly. As it is not a key element in starting your firm, the subject can be left there as far as this book is concerned. But take specialist advice well in advance if you think you may have to do it: an apparent redundancy can easily become an unfair dismissal if it is handled amateurishly. In any case, most employees are entitled to a redundancy payment, so a cost is attached to the decision.

10.15 Health and Safety at Work Act 1974

Very important: many small firms could be virtually closed down overnight if their working practices led to a serious accident. While the law does not normally expect you to do much more than lead the horse to water, under HASAWA you are expected to get him to drink as well, or at least to have a very good try. In practice, you should have safe working methods, safety training, and powerful sanctions for unsafe working (see section 10.11). It is not practicable to list all of the rules and regulations here as they are so numerous and there are special ones for many industries. The best plan is to consult the Factory Inspector before you set up and to get his advice on every aspect of your proposed operation. He will tell you what official notices must by law be displayed in your type of workshop and will advise on accident recording and reporting procedures. Do what he says and record it on file.

Insurance

11.1 Aims of this section

Insurance is something everyone can do without until disaster strikes. You can never insure against absolutely every possibility, and even if you could it would be ridiculously costly. The trick is to be carefully selective and to match costs to needs, updating your idea of what constitutes 'needs' as time goes on. Always enquire what reduction in premiums is available in return for accepting the first part of the risk.

11.2 A suggested approach

The new firm needs only two categories of insurance:

- The ones that the law requires (statutory)
- Insurance against catastrophe.

Only when you have made some money is it worth looking at other ways of spending it.

11.3 Statutory insurances

These include cover for employer's liability, motor vehicle, lifting tackle and pressure vessels. Some professional organisations insist on their members taking out professional liability policies, which is the next best thing to a legal requirement if you cannot practise unless you conform with their requirements. Other industries have had their own insurance arrangements confirmed by the law, like the travel agents' ABTA insurance, to protect customers' money in cases of insolvency. If you are unclear about any special requirements for your type of firm, talk to the trade associations and to a good commercial insurance broker. Remember that if you do not actually have any employees it could still be worth having cover for employer's liability in case of injury to a part-time helper, spouse, friend, schoolchild, or anyone else who might help out at some time.

11.4 Catastrophe insurances

These are policies that keep you or your family going even in the face of disaster. They include fire, flood, theft, death, disability, sickness, injury, loss of a partner's contribution, public liability, product liability (especially if you deal with the USA and likely to apply soon in the EC), and many more. The main thing is to buy what you can afford, while not falling below quite a high bare minimum.

In the early days, try to buy the cheapest variation of what you need – life insurance is the main area in which you can buy, and pay for, extras when all you really need is something basic but effective. Instead of a with-profits life policy (the most expensive kind, which also pays its salesmen the highest commission) you need a term policy – say, £100,000 cover for five or ten years. The amount should be calculated to clear up your debts in the event of your death, pay off the mortgage and provide a capital sum for the family; the period of cover should last for as long as you expect to be building your business. Partners should both be insured properly, to relieve the survivor of the responsibility to maintain his partner's widow. After a few years you can review the position and possibly take up other kinds of policies. According to your family and business circumstances there will be other forms of cover to consider.

11.5 Insurance packages

Most insurance companies offer standard policies for small firms which lump together the main types of cover you need. The contents or the extent of the cover under each heading may be negotiable. Thus you might be able to get reductions if some parts are cut out.

11.6 Insurance companies and their policies

If you insure for one thing and expect to be covered for another, you have only yourself to blame if the insurer will not pay up on your claim. So do not assume, but read the policy and understand it (which may be easier said than done). And always insure tangible property for full replacement cost, and insure everything. If you insure for half the value of your property, the insurer will probably pay only half of a claim. Especially important is the need to tell your insurer of changes to your circumstances – like using the family car for deliveries. (Have an accident when you are not covered and you could lose your licence as well.) Or using the house, garage or shed for your business. That is far from being a complete list. In matters as important as these it may be worth not just sending off a letter but asking for an acknowledgement and pressing until you get one.

11.7 Insurance brokers, agents and consultants

They may all look the same, but they are vastly different. 'Agents', 'consultants', or anyone but *registered brokers* are in business to sell insurances, pure and simple. The registered insurance broker, however, is required by his professional rules, backed by the law, to act on behalf of you, the client. He is your representative chasing the best deal for you from insurance companies. Although there are arguments for conducting some types of life insurance direct with the so-called 'non-tariff companies' (those that do not pay commission to brokers) the wide-ranging insurance needs of the small firm virtually dictate the use of a broker. Not all brokers are the same. You need one who specialises in insurance for industry and commerce rather than one whose main interest lies elsewhere. Get the benefit of his advice – lay your cards on the table, and let him tell you what he can do. Try this with a couple more, and settle for the one who seems to have your interests most at heart, perhaps helped by taking up references with satisfied customers. If he has any, he should be only too glad to give their names. He gets extra points if he insists on clearing it with the customers first.

Sources of Help

12.1 Aims of this section

Nearly everyone needs a shoulder to cry on at some time, and a friend, brother, brother-in-law or other relation can be invaluable in this respect. The owner of a bigger business could also be a useful ally, as he can bring new ways of looking at things – he has seen it all before. But the technical problems of running a firm also cause problems. Many people starting businesses make elementary errors precisely because they are in unfamiliar territory. Yet there are many agencies, mainly paid out of taxation or the rates, to help you spot pitfalls and sharpen up your ideas as well as to give technical help and advice. Some of the best are very good, yet do little advertising, so this section tries to describe what they do and where to find them, as well as how to use them. The main national organisations' addresses are shown in section 13. One characteristic of human beings is our extraordinary generosity to people who ask for advice or help. Your fellow man will help, but only if asked.

12.2 Selecting a consultant or adviser

Ask around among business contacts to see who they use, and who they would not touch at any price. Take a look at all the bodies available in your area, meet the people and see who looks right for you. Then ask for the names of a couple of people that they have helped in the early stages of business whom you could telephone for a chat to see exactly how their users find they can help. (Be careful not to make it sound too much like taking up a reference.) Their attitude, and the 'referees' that they have supplied, should point you to the one source that you can rely on and use in depth. He or she will not necessarily be the most flattering of the people you meet, but will be interested in the project, quick on the uptake, have useful knowledge of a broad range of businesses, have management experience in the private sector, and above all will not try to impress you with his or her own importance or have a black-and-white attitude to everything.

12.3 Using an adviser

No adviser can run your business for you: beware the one who tries to. All advice should be listened to, but you take the decisions and the responsibility, so no advice should be taken undiluted if you do not believe it is right and understand clearly why it is recommended. Any adviser worth his salt will not seek to dominate, but will work with you to help you reach the best decisions. It is therefore important for you to give him room, so do not dominate him, either. As the best of these people are usually very busy, they tend to deal verbally with the sort of general enquiry you will make at the outset, rather than writing a report to you.

Keep a notepad at the ready and jot down the points that the adviser makes, and the names and phone numbers that he will give you. Ask what his specialities are and what back-up he has on areas where he is weak, and how deeply involved he gets with his clients. Some agencies offer little more than one or two general interviews at the start of your enterprise, some will act virtually as guide, philosopher and friend, helping you to found your business and orchestrate its development. All the time you need to encourage an atmosphere of openness and trust. Your secrets will usually be kept but, more importantly, the adviser cannot do his job if you hold back vital information. If you hedge or do not do what you have agreed to, he will lose interest and spend his scarce time on other, more rewarding, clients.

12.4 Private sector advisers

Your accountant and solicitor have been mentioned elsewhere as advisers to be used for their great strengths in their own specialist fields. Brief them fully, and ask what they can do for you. Your bank manager, too, can be useful and is ignored at your peril. He has seen more business failures and successes than most, and the better type will have wise words for you. There are the consultancy groups who, large or small, will work for anyone who pays their fee. Unfortunately, they are a bit costly at several hundred pounds per day. Because this type of expertise is so crucially important to small firms, various public sector bodies have set up subsidised consultancies to make it available more affordably. Finally, there are the independent business consultants, some of whom are absolutely excellent, and cost considerably less than their larger brethren. Equally, there are at large people who insinuate themselves into businesses on the pretext of helping them to solve pressing problems, and proceed systematically to defraud. Many of them are clever enough to do it so as to get away with it. That does not mean that independent consultants should be dismissed out of hand, but that at least three satisfactory references should be obtained. The cost of using a consultant could be offset by grants introduced by the Department of Trade and Industry's 'Enterprise Initiative'.

12.5 Public sector organisations

These fall into two divisions: nationally organised, and locally organised. Local organisations are usually based on county councils, district councils, colleges, polytechnics and universities, development corporations, chambers of commerce, and local enterprise agencies. To locate them all you need to do is phone around, not forgetting your public library, and make up a list. National organisations include the Welsh Development Agency, the Scottish Development Agency, the Small Firms Service of the Department of Trade and Industry, and the Rural Development Commission's Business Service (formerly CoSIRA). As the last two are the most widely available, brief sections on them follow. If your product is related to agriculture the Ministry of Agriculture's Agricultural Development and Advisory Service (ADAS) may help. Some people use these advisers as sounding-boards for their ideas, and for a periodic check-up on progress as a form of preventive medicine for their firm.

12.6 The Small Firms Service

This has a UK-wide network of regional offices which can be reached by dialling 100 and asking for Freefone Enterprise. They offer a telephone enquiry answering service on any business matter, for which no charge is made. In addition, they have a team of (mainly retired) businessmen to whom they pay a small fee in return for their offering their experience to small firms. The first few sessions are free, after which they charge £30 per meeting. Also, through the Production Engineering Research Association, they can help with technical problems.

12.7 Rural Development Commission's Business Service (formerly CoSIRA)

The Development Commission's origins go back over 60 years when the first official attempt was made to help small, non-farming firms outside the main towns. Today it offers a service of great breadth and depth to small business. Every English county has a local office, staffed by a business generalist, backed up by a voluntary steering committee of influential local people concerned to help small businesses in the country. It also has a team of 100 full-time management and technical specialists who can be used for advice and trouble-shooting, as well as training. They run nearly 50 short courses (half day to five days) on various technical and management subjects. The advisory specialists cover practically everything a small firm needs, from accounting and marketing through to designing workshops, advising on microcomputers, and training you to weld, plus a great deal more which cannot be listed here.

It operates in English villages and towns of up to 10,000 population, and gives priority to 'Rural Development Areas', where it can offer extra help.

12.8 Some you might not have thought of

Trading Standards Departments, which used to be known as Weights and Measures, and the Health and Safety Executive (formerly Factory Inspectorate) can be a great help to any small firm. Like most enforcement agencies, they prefer to set you on the right road rather than let you go wrong and then prosecute you. If you depend on tourist traffic, the regional Tourist Boards could help. Local chambers of commerce and small firms' clubs offer informal advice. Polytechnics and universities are sometimes stuck for projects for business students, and could do research work for you free of charge. Suppliers, customers and even competitors can be helpful, too.

Computers and the New Firm

13.1 Aims of this section

The ever-falling cost of computers, and the extravagant claims made for their powers by some advertisers, have led many a new business to invest in one. Too often the machines are seen a few months later, covered in dust and under a desk. The owner, sadder but wiser, bears the scars of too many late nights spent unsuccessfully trying to get the system to do what he wanted it to do. Towards the end he lowered his sights and tried to get it just to do what the instruction manual said it would, but even that modest ambition failed. In the end he had to give up and devise manual systems to keep his records. This section aims to help you to avoid this sort of failure by explaining the limitations, as well as the capabilities, of computers in the very small firm. It also tells you how to identify whether or not a computer will be more of a handicap than a help, and, if you do decide to go ahead, how to increase the chances of your installation being successful.

13.2 What you don't need to know or to learn

You do not need to understand anything but the bare minimum about electronics or programming. You do not need to learn any of the programming languages.

13.3 When to consider getting a computer

If your operation is straightforward, simple, is unlikely to grow, and does not involve much complexity, it is likely that a computer will be much more trouble than it is worth. Firms which display complexity, in the sense meant here, have one or more of the following characteristics:

- many customers or suppliers
- many orders
- many quotations, most or all of which use standard elements
- large number of items in stock requiring frequent reordering
- much or frequent financial analysis
- large number of calculations, especially if they involve formulae

- many agents or employees
- complicated records
- lots of drafting and revision of documents
- frequent need to present numerical information in the form of charts
- many personalised letters, quotations or other documents.

There can be other, specialised, reasons why a computer can help, which the individual entrepreneur will know of as part of his knowledge of his industry.

In general, a firm which has to deal with any of the problems listed above ought to be looking at a computer. If a computer is desirable to deal with a special need, it is worth thinking of getting it to do other routines of which it is capable, such as the payroll, for instance, even though the workforce may not be big enough to justify it on its own.

Otherwise, the sensible thing to do is to heave a sigh of relief. You will not have to spend most of your precious leisure time and a great deal of working time that you can ill afford on getting to grips with computers. Instead you can keep your records on simple card-indexes, in books and in other 'user-friendly' ways.

13.4 How the computer can help

In theory it is possible to get a programmer to write a program which will get the computer to do exactly what you want – to reproduce your manual methods. Regrettably, the cost would be astronomical. Therefore you have to think in terms not of getting exactly what you want, but of getting as close as you can within the limitations of the off-the-shelf programs (or software as they are called, in contrast to the hardware, or equipment). Software exists for all kinds of jobs: there are literally hundreds of payroll programs, for instance, which will calculate each employee's wages, NI, tax and pension contributions and even work out exactly how many notes and coins of which denominations you have to draw from the bank to make up the pay-packets.

In addition to the special-purpose programs there are the three main workhorses which most firms can put to work in some way. They are databases, spreadsheets and word processors.

13.5 Databases

A database is really a clever version of a card-index. It can carry the sort of information you would put on to record cards. If we take as an example a set of customer records, the obvious information for them to carry is name, address, telephone, dates of visits, what ordered, value and dates of purchases, names and positions of contacts and so on. What sets the database apart from the card-index is the facility instantaneously to:

- sort the records into any order you like: they will already be in alphabetical order by customer names, perhaps, but you can change that to descending order by value of purchases last year if you want to (and then back again)
- perform calculations, such as adding up the value of sales to all customers in one county last year
- perform conditional operations, such as finding the value of sales to customers who have not bought product X and have more than three branches of which one is in Staffordshire.

Setting up a database requires a huge investment of time and effort. It takes time to learn how to set it up; it takes time to enter the information; and it takes time to learn how to extract the information you want. Like all programs, databases are ruthless in requiring you to follow precisely every single step of complicated instructions. If you miss out even one comma the whole thing can throw out garbage or refuse to work.

Critical factors in selecting a database include its overall capacity – whether it fits in your machine, and whether it is big enough to take your records, now and in the future; its ease of use; and the speed with which it performs the routines you will use (some can be desperately slow).

What is described here as a 'relational' database, in which the different kinds of information on each record can be related to one other. To be avoided by the serious business user is the simpler sort which is incapable of relational work.

13.6 Spreadsheets

A spreadsheet is like two vast sheets of squared paper overlaying one another and reacting together. On the top sheet you can write words and numbers, which are normally visible on the computer screen. You can place the computer's screen over any part of the spreadsheet that you want to view at any particular time. On the lower sheet you can write formulae which act on the figures on the top sheet. If you want to look at the formulae, you can. A simple example of how it can be used is to give quotations. A landscape gardener is often asked to give a price for laying slabs, so he programs his spreadsheet to do the calculations automatically. He puts in the number of square metres to be covered on this job, and the computer looks up the price of hardcore, aggregate, sand, surface materials and labour which the owner has entered previously (and can change at will), works out how much of each is required, multiplies them out and totals them up, then adds the VAT to give the answer. Someone who knew what they were doing, perhaps after a few months of playing with spreadsheets, would set up the entire example above in under an hour, including headings and the introductory words necessary. Having done so, he or she would never have to do such sums themselves again.

While all spreadsheets look pretty big at first glance, it is important to check that their dimensions are right for what you have in mind. For example, a program which allows 100 columns across sounds very large. But a firm which wants to keep track of its targets and achievements week by week will need at least 107 columns: one for each of the weekly targets plus an annual total (53), the same for the outcomes (another 53) plus one for the headings down the left hand side. As an alternative it could run the two sets of figures and their labels in 54 columns by putting one set above the other, instead of side-by-side. But there are so many spreadsheets to choose from that this sort of compromise may not be necessary.

13.7 Word processors

A word processor is a typewriter which allows you to see what you have typed before printing, and change it if need be. Many include spelling-checkers (though some disapprove of non-American English!). To the amateur typist they are a godsend – this writer would not be without one – for he can eliminate his mistakes so easily, hack documents around until they look right, move chunks of text from one place to another, experiment with layout and so on. Another thing it can do is to link up with spreadsheets and databases to bring in information from them. An example might be a personalised mailshot aimed at getting customers to buy 20 per cent more than they did last year. The customer's address would be taken off the database to head up the word processor letter, the buyer's name would likewise be lifted into the word processor for the greeting, and last year's purchases would also be switched across. If you want to be really clever you can perform some calculations on spreadsheet to see how much bonus the customer would earn, and pop that into the letter too. Some word processors will even do the sums themselves. This sort of switching-about of information between different programs is vastly easier if the three are bought as a 'suite' in which they are designed to talk to one another. However, compromise may be necessary if this is important to you. Not every element in the suite may deliver the full specification you require.

A further argument in favour of suites is that they may allow you to break off in the middle of one job to do another without a lot of rigmarole. If an urgent customer query comes up in the middle of some word processing it can be tedious to have to save the incomplete document, go into database, come out again and reload.

The factor which most people find important in selecting a word processor is whether it will do all the jobs they want it to, and only then how easy it is to use. They reason that you can always learn difficult routines, but you can never extend the program's power. The sole exception to the ease-of-use criterion is that nowadays everyone has a right – in the writer's opinion – to WYSIWYG (What You See Is What You Get). In the bad old days, when you wanted to switch between different typefaces or do other things within one document, you had to write a lot of instructions in computerese, and these appeared on the screen in the middle of your text. It upset layout and appearance. But modern word processors conceal the instructions, so that what appears on the screen is what you will see on the page. But there are still some of the old-type programs on the market.

13.8 Selecting your system

You find out which program suits your operation best by:

- carefully specifying exactly what you want the program to do
- comparing the specifications of each program in your price and capacity range with what you are looking for
- reading the reviews in magazines to see what problems the experts have unearthed, and how they compare with other programs of the same type
- only then going to see what it looks like on the screen in the dealer's showroom.

Contrary to most people's understanding, the software is the thing you really spend time and trouble to find out about. Hardware is a lot less important, in the sense that there is not a lot to choose between the machines (except price, reliability and how happy you feel with the keyboard). The only exception to the general rule is that some programs are now so cheap that you may feel you can afford to buy one or two to play with, without the rigour of the selection process described above.

The hardware to pick is really up to you, as long as it is truly 100 per cent IBM compatible (anything that is less compatible than that may not run the most popular and most readily available software). Some people feel happy only if they have the genuine IBM machine, but they pay for the peace of mind. Others are happier if they spend less, especially as that does not necessarily mean that they get a worse machine. Perhaps the most important factor is dealer back-up. If your local dealer is likely to be around for a time and knows what he is up to, it is almost worth specifying the brand that he stocks. Then when (not if) things go wrong you have someone local to pull you out of the mire.

Your printer is worth a little thought. Printers fall into two categories: daisywheel and dot matrix.

Daisywheel printers carry a piece of type on the end of an arm, the entire alphabet being carried on arms radiating out from a centre: the whole thing is circular and looks a bit like a daisy. If you tell it to print Y, the Y arm will whizz round to the top of the wheel and be hit by a hammer, making it print Y like a conventional typewriter.

A dot matrix is very different. The shape of the letter is made up by many tiny pins which move in and out according to the letter to be printed, and then hit the ribbon to print it. The choice is governed by your printing needs. Daisywheels print just like good-quality typewriters. However, they are slow: 20 characters per second (cps) might be typical. While that sounds pretty quick, it does mean that you wait for about a minute for a page of A4 to be printed. Also, if you want to change print-style, say to italic and back again in the middle of a sentence, you have to change the daisywheel to italic and back. Dot matrix is fast; 160 cps is typical in 'draft' mode (the computer type obviously made up from separate dots), which is all you need for drafting and for internal documents. Changing typeface in mid-document is simple. Switching to NLQ (near letter-quality) can be done simply for external documents, when the speed comes down to around 25 or 30 cps. The appearance of NLQ is improving all the time (though some are still pretty ropey) and the best are as good as an average daisywheel. Their versatility is leading them to race away from daisywheels.

13.9 Computer manuals and other problems

In theory, the manuals which come with the machine and with the software are the user's best friend and his main learning tool. Unfortunately, many manuals are the opposite, due to sloppiness by the firms which produce them. It does not take much imagination to see how you would feel if the following happens to you. You take the system home on a Friday night, meaning to spend a couple of hours before bed writing a couple of routines to use during the following week. You follow the instructions exactly but it refuses to work. You check everything thoroughly in both software and hardware manuals, but still get nowhere. At 2 am you go to bed, frustrated. You wake up tired and irritable, your mood not helped by complaints from the family that they cannot use the dining-room because of all your mess. You spend most of the rest of the weekend in a state of increasing hopelessness, and do none of the jobs you meant to tackle. On Monday you ring the supplier, who asks three questions about what you did. It turns out that the vital thing you did not do they have known about for a year, but have not got round to correcting in the manuals. And that is not the worst the machines can do – the manuals tell you to record what you have done quite frequently. That is because some freak event in the electricity supply can cause the machine to freeze up, refusing to respond to any commands. The only thing to do is switch off, then on again. Simple enough, but you lose everything you have not recorded, which is not funny at the end of five or six hours' work. The way to reduce the risk of a freeze, incidentally, is to spend £30 or so on a device that smooths out the accidental 'spikes' in the mains supply.

You may be offered a choice of screen, usually between monochrome (which can be green or, usually for a few pounds more, amber) and colour. The latter looks pretty, but can cost £200 extra. When you have spent several hours looking at it you could find it more disturbing than helpful. Many people believe that it is preferable to spend another £30 or so over the basic monochrome price to get a high-resolution mono display. High-resolution colour displays are available, but very expensive.

You will be presented with a choice of disk-drive. Most people believe that this is the area in which it is worth pushing the boat out. Business users cannot afford the delay that a single floppy disk imposes. With that system, you spend several minutes loading into the machine the programs and data that you want to use before you can start work, and there can be further fuss every time you want to do something with the program. A twin floppy system is better but far from ideal. Anyone who has used a hard disk swears by it. Instead of keeping all the instructions and information outside the machine and loading it in when you want to use it, a hard disk keeps it permanently on hand in the machine.

An inescapable expense is a maintenance contract. They usually cost annually about 10 per cent of the equipment's value, which is not cheap. But having your business out of action while the engineer gives priority to his contract customers incurs a cost.

Your Business Plan

14.1 Aims of this section

A great deal of this book is given over to extolling the idea of planning ahead to create the future you want. In many places it advocates getting those plans down on paper, partly so that you can see what you think and criticise it objectively; partly so that you have a record of where you are trying to go, to make it easy to judge how well you are doing and provide early warning of unscheduled departures from the route; and partly to ensure that all the pieces fit together (that you are not planning to sell more than you can make, for example). Much of that sort of planning is often left written in longhand, and some of it may be comprehensible to its writer alone. This section aims to help you to take that information, add to it further facts that you are expected to supply, and present the whole thing in a form that ought to satisfy a complete stranger, sitting in an office, who knows next to nothing about your sort of firm. Increasingly, small firms are expected to do that: and if they do not they can miss out on quite a lot of the help that is available.

14.2 Who wants your plan and why?

The new business will find more and more that it is asked to submit a business plan to support its application for loans, grants or even just a lease on a building. Those who make such requests are not busybodies. Even if they were, it matters little, for if they have something that you need it makes sense to go at least part of the way to meet them. The plan written for the owner's personal use is rarely suitable, for it uses unexplained jargon and abbreviations and takes a great deal of knowledge for granted.

The reason why such people will call for a business plan falls under several headings. Among other things it is expected to:

- demonstrate that the applicant has a coherent plan
- show that the applicant can read, write, do sums and understands at least something of what running a business entails
- illustrate how the business will establish itself and show that its chances of survival and success are good

- show how risky areas are to be made safe
- communicate that good use will be made of the reader's resources
- impress and reassure.

Nobody wants to provide money or premises to someone who seems likely to go broke and cause them a lot of trouble. Everyone wants to see vibrantly healthy firms in their patch.

14.3 What goes into a business plan?

The plans of a large firm, or a smaller one that is involved in particularly turbulent makets, may comprise very many pages and sections. The new, small firm rarely has to go to those lengths. Indeed, there is a lot of merit in keeping it very simple: plans stretching to hundreds, or even dozens, of pages quickly lose the reader. In one sense you are engaged here in salesmanship, so don't drone on about how much you know, but instead give the reader what he is looking for.

The purpose of the plan is to answer the key questions that everyone will ask: who, what, why, when, where and how? To help readers to get their answers it makes sense to divide the plan up into sections which tell:

- the background to the project
- what your aims are
- relevant information about the market, production and finance
- what you will do if things don't go according to plan

... and answer the 'who, what, why' etc questions under each heading.

The project's background: up to two pages
In general terms, what is happening in the industry you plan to enter (market size, competition, structures, prices etc)?
What is the opportunity?
How do you plan to exploit it?
Is it a 'flash in the pan'?
What are the qualifications of each participant?
Effects of outside factors (commodity shortages, social/demographic/technological change, public attitudes, legal controls etc).

Aims of the project: one page
What is your long-term aim for the business?
What markers will it pass at what times on the way there?

The market: up to two pages
How is the market structured: users, distributors, trade margins and discounts, competitors?

169

Do any special financing conventions apply?

What seasonal or trade fluctuations are typical in the trade?

How do you fit in: why should they buy from you?

How does your pricing compare with competitors'?

How will you sell your goods; who will do that work, over what area, and by what method?

What is your sales forecast for each of the next five years?

How big a market share does this represent (the smaller the better, or it might look optimistic)?

What is your sales forecast for each month of the first year?

What promotional support do you propose and at what cost?

How will the product be packaged and presented?

Where will you get the people, how will they be trained and controlled?

Production: up to two pages

What production processes will be conducted in-house and which outside, and why?

What knowledge do you have of these matters and how will you cover any shortcomings?

What premises will you get and at what cost?

How will you know product costs, and what are they?

How many productive hours per person per week are you assuming, and for how many weeks a year?

Which process represents a bottleneck, and how will you deal with any limitations it imposes?

How readily available is essential labour, and at what cost?

What training is needed, how will it be provided and at what cost?

How will you control production?

How will you control quality?

How will continuity of supply of components be assured?

How will component stocks be controlled?

(NB: The last two questions are only for firms which are critically dependent on particular components or suppliers, or where stocks of components represent a major part of their financial requirements.)

Finance: four pages or so (there are several tables)

How profitable will the firm be?

(Answered by a *profit and loss projection*.)

What finance will be needed when, and for what purposes?

(This question is best dealt with by providing a *capital budget*, showing how much is needed for each of the main capital items; and a *cash flow forecast*, showing temporary shortfalls and surpluses of working capital.)

Where will the money come from?
(This is the *funding budget*, showing who contributes how much and in what form.)

What security is offered to lenders?
Opening and closing *balance sheet projections* can be shown for the start and finish of each trading year. They answer the question: how much better off does the firm expect to be as time moves on?

What strengths and weaknesses are displayed in these figures, and how will weaknesses be dealt with?

What is the projected break-even point for each year, and how far above it does the firm expect to trade?
(That shows how much leeway there is for accidents and emergencies.)

Administration: what financial records will be kept, how and by whom?

Control: what financial controls will be exercised and by whom?

People: who will be required, how available are they and at what cost?

Clearly, most people who wish to write this sort of business plan will need help, especially with the financial projections. It is always a good idea to have somebody to help: it greatly increases the chance of removing embarrassing errors. Watch out for the lazy adviser who puts it all on computer and projects your monthly sales as exactly one-twelfth of your forecast for the year. It sticks out like a sore thumb to your reader, who is tempted to conclude that it is all as slapdash as that. Remember – bank managers and others have seen a lot of these plans and can most readily spot insincerity. They are also very keen on the idea that you should understand the plan. A response to questions – and there will always be questions – that suggests you don't understand what the figures mean will not go down well. That might explain why some readers are in two minds about plans prepared by prestige accountants. On the one hand they know that a professional job has been done; on the other they may suspect that some well-paid wise guy is trying to put one over them. All in all they probably feel happiest with something you have prepared but which has been checked by an accountant (who may well have helped with the number-crunching).

It is also worth subjecting the plan to critical scrutiny at the draft stage from someone who is used to writing or judging these documents. There is plenty of help on hand from the small-business agencies, both by way of preparation and constructive criticism.

14.4 Presentation

Appearances ought not to matter as much as they do, perhaps. But it is an inescapable fact that those reading your plan will be strongly influenced by what it looks like: the cover, the layout, the quality of paper and the standard of typing. For those reasons it is worth going to a professional typist who has a good-quality machine. If he or she cannot supply a cover of the sort you want, your local commercial stationer can. While you are at it, it will not cost much more to have several copies printed.

Useful Names and Addresses

Advisory, Conciliation and
Arbitration Service (ACAS)
27 Wilton Street
London SW1X 7AZ
01-210 3600

Agricultural Development
Advisory Service
Ministry of Agriculture, Fisheries
and Food
Great Westminster House
Horseferry Road
London SW1P 2AB
01-216 6311

Alliance of Small Firms and Self
Employed People
33 The Green
Calne
Wiltshire SN11 8DJ
0249 817003

BBC External Services
PO Box 76
Bush House
Strand
London WC2B 4PU
01-240 3456

British Agents' Register
24 Mount Parade
Harrogate HG1 1BP
0423 60608

British Franchise Association
Franchise Chambers
75a Bell Street
Henley-on-Thames
Oxfordshire RG9 2BD
0491 578049

British Institute of Management
Small Firms Information Service
Management House
Cottingham Road
Corby
Northamptonshire NN17 1TT
0536 20422

British Insurance Brokers Association
BIBA House
14 Bevis Marks
London EC3N 7AT
01-623 9043

British Overseas Trade Board
1 Victoria Street
London SW1H 0ET
01-215 7877

British Standards Institution
(Technical Help to Exporters)
Linford Wood
Milton Keynes MK14 6LE
0908 220022

British Technology Group
101 Newington Causeway
London SE1 6BU
01-403 6666

Building Research Establishment
Bucknalls Lane
Watford WD2 7JR
and
Kelvin Road
Glasgow

Central Office of Information
Hercules Road
London SE1 7DU
01-928 2345

Chartered Institute of Patent Agents
Staple Inn Buildings
London WC1V 7PX
01-405-9450

Companies Registration Offices:
Companies House
Crown Way
Maindy
Cardiff CF4 3UZ
0222 388588

Companies House
55 City Road
London EC1Y 1BB
01-253 9393

102 George Street
Edinburgh EH2 3DJ
031-225 5774

IDB House
64 Chichester Street
Belfast BT1 4JX
0232 234488

Co-operative Development Agency
Broadmead House
21 Panton Street
London SW1Y 4DR
01-839 2988

Country Landowners' Association
16 Belgrave Square
London SW1X 8PQ
01-235 0511

Crafts Council
8 Waterloo Place
London SW1Y 4AU
01-930 4811

Department of Employment
Head Office
Caxton House
Tothill Street
London SW1H 9NF
01-213 3000

Design Council
28 Haymarket
London SW1Y 4SU
01-839 8000

Durham University Business School
Mill Hill Lane
Durham DH1 3LB
091-374 2000

Equipment Leasing Association
18 Upper Grosvenor Street
London W1X 9PB
01-491 2783

EXBO (Export Buying Offices
Association)
Avon House
360 Oxford Street
London W1A 4BX
01-493 8141

Export Credits Guarantee
Department
Export House
50 Ludgate Hill
London EC4M 7AY
01-382 7000

Finance Houses Association
18 Upper Grosvenor Street
London W1X 9PB
01-491 2783

Highlands and Islands Development
Board
Bridge House
Bank Street
Inverness IV1 1QR
0463 234171

Hotel Catering and Institutional
Management Association
191 Trinity Road
London SW17 7HN
01-672 4251

Industrial and Commercial Finance
Corporation (3i)
91 Waterloo Road
London SE1 8XP
01-928 7822

Institute of Directors
116 Pall Mall
London SW1Y 5ED
01-839 1233

Institute of Marketing
Moor Hall
Cookham
Maidenhead SL6 9QH
06285 24922

Institute of Patentees and Inventors
Suite 505A
Triumph House
189 Regent Street
London W1R 7WF
01-242 7812

Institute of Trade Mark Agents
Canterbury House
4th Floor
2-6 Sydenham Road
Croydon CR0 9XE
01-686 2052

London Enterprise Agency
(LENTA)
4 Snow Hill
London EC1A 2BS
01-236 3000

Manufacturers' Agents' Association
Lonsdale House
7-11 High Street
Reigate
Surrey RH2 9AA
07372 40141

Mid Wales Development Board
Ladywell House
Newtown

Powys SY16 1JB
0686 626965

National Computing Centre Ltd
Oxford Road
Manchester M1 7ED
061-228 6333

National Farmers' Union
Agriculture House
Knightsbridge
London SW1X 7NJ
01-235 5077

National Federation of Self
Employed and Small Businesses
32 St Anne's Road West
Lytham St Anne's
Lancashire FY8 1NY
0253 720911

and

140 Lower Marsh
London SE1 7AE
01-928 9272

Northern Ireland Development
Agency
100 Belfast Road
Holywood
County Down
02317 4232

Northern Ireland Local Enterprise
Development Unit
Ledu House
Upper Galwally
Belfast BT8 4TB
0232 491031

Production Engineering Research
Assocation
Melton Mowbray
Leicestershire LE13 0PB
0664 64133

Rural Development Commission
Business Service (formerly CoSIRA)
141 Castle Street
Salisbury SP1 3TP
0722 336255
Local offices: see telephone book.

Scottish Development Agency
120 Bothwell Street
Glasgow G2 7JP
041-248 2700
and
(Small Business Division)
21 Bothwell Street
Glasgow G2 6NR
041-248 7806
and
Rosebery House
Haymarket Terrace
Edinburgh EH12 5EZ
031-337 9595

Small Business Bureau
32 Smith Square
London SW1P 3HH
01-222 9000

Small Firms Centres
All centres can be contacted by
dialling 100 and asking for Freefone
Enterprise.

   9th Floor, Alpha Tower
   Suffolk Street
   Queensway
   Birmingham B1 1TT
   021-643 3344

   6th Floor, The Pithay
   Bristol BS1 2NB
   0272 294546

   Carlyle House
   Carlyle Road
   Cambridge CB4 3DN
   0223 63312

16 St David's House
Wood Street
Cardiff CF1 1ER
0222 396116

120 Bothwell Street
Glasgow G2 6NR
041-248 6014

1 Park Row
City Square
Leeds LS1 5NR
0532 445151

Graeme House
Derby Square
Liverpool L3 9HJ
051-236 5756

Ebury Bridge House
2-18 Ebury Bridge Road
London SW1W 8QD
01-730 8451

3rd Floor
26-28 Deansgate
Manchester M3 1RH
061-832 5282

15th Floor
Cale Cross House
156 Pilgrim Street
Newcastle upon Tyne NE1 6PZ
091-232 5353

Severns House
Middle Pavement
Nottingham NG1 7DW
0602 581205

Business and Technology Centre
Bessemer Centre
Stevenage SG1 2DX
0438 743377

Trade Marks Registry
State House
66–71 High Holborn
London WC1R 4TP

Union of Independent Companies
44–46 Fleet Street
London EC4Y 1BN
01-589 9305

Venture Capital Report
Boston Road
Henley-on-Thames
Oxon RG9 1DY
0491 579999

Welsh Development Agency
Treforest Industrial Estate
Pontypridd
Mid Glamorgan CF37 5UT
044 385 2666

Appendices

Budgeting Exercise: Yule Fuel Company

John Smith had worked for many years in a large sawmill. Being brought up to dislike waste, and being a bit of an amateur engineer, he had been experimenting with methods of converting sawmill woodchips and sawdust into logs of fuel. Disposing of it was a problem for the mill, who could get rid of it only by selling it cheaply to horse and pet owners as a litter material. While it made some money for them, it was a nuisance to deal with the many visitors.

An imminent change in working methods at the mill meant that John's job would cease to exist in six months' time. The manager was sad to have to tell him, for John had been a good worker, but he could offer no alternative employment and competition meant that there was no room for passengers.

Once he and his wife had recovered from the shock they started to consider the alternatives. John's neighbour was the first to suggest that he should start up on his own. The logs were coming out well now from the machine he had developed; and many of the people whom he knew owned wood-burning stoves and were complaining that Dutch elm disease meant no more cheap fuel. In his part of the country the 1987 gales had not blown down many trees.

John researched the market carefully and concluded that he could go ahead. People reported favourably on how the fuel burned, they liked his price, and all the garages and shops he approached said that they would stock it. The mill was happy to let him take all of their waste at £2 per tonne. He would not need it all at first, but reckoned that he could still turn a penny by selling some to the pet owners whose supply would dry up. That would be a bonus, though; his main concern was the logs, and he sat down to prepare a financial plan.

The facts he had established were:

Material costs	Dust: £2 per tonne (1000 kg) paid on collection
	Bags: 50p per 25 kg bag, cash on delivery
Rent	£2000 pa, paid January, April, July, October
Rates	£1000 pa, paid April and October
Wages	£500 per month
Transport	£200 per month

Electricity	£300 per quarter, paid March, June, September, December
Post and phone	£100 per quarter, paid March, June, September and December
Insurance	£500 pa, paid in January
Packages	25 kg bags, selling for £3
Customers pay	Half pay cash on delivery, half pay two months after delivery
Output	500 bags per month (6000 pa)
Orders	500 bags per month January to March, 300 April to September, 800 October to December (5700 pa)

The equipment John has assembled is worth about £2000 and will last some five years. So he allows for depreciation at the rate of £2000 ÷ 5 = £400 pa.

YULE FUEL COMPANY

Product cost per bag

Materials $\dfrac{25}{1000} \times £2$	=	£0.05
Packaging	=	£0.50
Total cost		£0.55
Selling price	=	£3.00
Value added	=	£2.45

So the first arithmetic John does suggests that materials costing him 55p can be sold for £3, leaving him with £2.45 per bag to pay the costs of the business and to give him a wage. Now he wants to know whether the quantity he expects to sell will actually meet his costs and earn him a living. He draws up a Profit and Loss Budget, as shown opposite.

So it looks as if the business should pay John's modest wage, but not make much profit in its first year. He might expect it to make more in the second year, because 300 bags from the stocks he builds up this summer will be available to be sold after Christmas: this year he could sell only the 500 bags that he can make each month, despite having orders for more. But it is still a slim margin of safety, as it gives him only £6000 of wages plus £65 of profit, out of which interest and tax may have to be paid. So he may need to rethink the proposal rather radically, or even abandon it in its present form.

YULE FUEL COMPANY

Profit and Loss Budget year ended ...

	£	£
Sales		17,100
Materials: Bags	2,850	
Dust	285	3,135
Value added		13,965
Overheads		
Rent and rates	3,000	
Wages	6,000	
Transport	2,400	
Electricity	1,200	
Post and phone	400	
Insurance	500	
Depreciation	400	13,900
Profit before interest and tax		65

He decides to persevere with the arithmetic at least. The next part of the plan is to produce the cash flow budget (shown on page 184). Remember that he will keep on making 500 bags a month throughout the year, although he will not be selling them all during the summer.

The last line of the cash flow budget, in effect, forecasts the bank balance. It makes sorry reading. The debt mounts until it gets to practically £3000 in September and then reduces. On the whole, we might conclude that this is not too bright an idea. It sounded fine at first, making over £2 profit per bag; the equipment is all bought and paid for; and the redundancy cheque will more than cover the firm's financial needs. But as John himself now sees, a little more analysis shows up the flaws; this is no place to invest his redundancy money.

He might now look at how the plan can be changed. The main problems it suffers from are its seasonal nature and inflexible output, so that stocks have to be built up during the summer while little is sold; and the high overheads in relation to turnover. You do not need to work out the break-even point to see that it is a fragile proposition. The idea that £65 might be left over out of £17,000, if all the other forecast figures come true, allows little room for error. It is a reward which is more than likely expected from a conventional investment of the same amount, but a building society would be far safer.

YULE FUEL COMPANY

Cash Flow Budget year ended . . .

	J	F	M	A	M	J	J	A	S	O	N	D
Invoiced Sales	1,500	1,500	1,500	900	900	900	900	900	900	2,400	2,400	2,400
Receipts												
Cash	750	750	750	450	450	450	450	450	450	1,200	1,200	1,200
Debtors	—	—	750	750	750	450	450	450	450	450	450	1,200
(a) Total receipts	750	750	1,500	1,200	1,200	900	900	900	900	1,650	1,650	2,400
Payments												
Rent and rates	500			500			500			500		
Wages	500	500	500	500	500	500	500	500	500	500	500	500
Transport	200	200	200	200	200	200	200	200	200	200	200	200
Electricity			300			300			300			300
Post and phone			100			100			100			100
Insurance	500											
Raw material	275	275	275	275	275	275	275	275	275	275	275	275
(b) Total payments	1,975	975	1,375	1,475	975	1,375	1,475	975	1,375	1,475	975	1,375
(a) – (b) Receipts less Payments	(1,225)	(225)	125	(275)	225	(475)	(575)	(75)	(475)	175	675	1,025
Cumulative	(1,225)	(1,450)	(1,325)	(1,600)	(1,375)	(1,850)	(2,425)	(2,500)	(2,975)	(2,800)	(2,125)	(1,100)

On the other hand, the building society would only pay interest on the loan, whereas the business does plan to pay John a very basic wage. So what do we conclude? Well, everyone's circumstances and attitudes are different. Some people would run a mile from a proposition like this; others would find it acceptable. Insofar as one person can make an objective judgement, my opinion is that the risks of self-employment need to be better rewarded than this. If John can possibly get a job and put his money in a safer place he would be well advised to do so.

Now, if he could raise prices by £1 – or 99p – a bag, the picture would be transformed. Provided, of course, that the volume does not fall much. You might like to work out what price level would give the income that would satisfy your personal income and profit requirements. If you were doing this in real life you would then try to reassess the size of the market at the new price. Who knows, far from shrinking, it might grow!

Help for Small Businesses

The following organisations are some of those which offer help of various sorts for small firms. If you are in any doubt as to how to get in touch with them, your local Rural Development Commission's Business Service office or Small Firms Centre should be able to tell you. Their addresses appear in section 15.

Banks. Most banks publish free booklets on many aspects of starting and running a business, give away forms on which to do financial planning, and run newsletters.

British Overseas Trade Board. This government body gives leaflets, help and advice on exporting.

Chambers of commerce. Joining the local chamber can be a good way of making business contacts, as well as giving you access to a library and information service, help with exporting, and a voice in representations to public authorities.

Chambers of trade. Quite separate from the chamber of commerce, which usually serves industry and commerce, the chamber of trade does similar work for retailers and wholesalers.

Co-operative Development Agencies. These organisations give help and advice to people wishing to set up a co-operative venture.

County courts. They give away a booklet on making claims for payment of debts of up to £2000, and what to do if such a claim is made against you.

Customs and Excise VAT offices. Their staff offer advice on all aspects of VAT and dispense free booklets.

Department of Trade and Industry. This government department is the main source of grants for industry. Its regional offices can advise on every facet of their help, and their Small Firms Centres translate it into terms that help small businesses. The latter also give advice and information on setting up and running a small firm, and offer useful free booklets.

Development agencies (for Scotland, Wales and Northern Ireland). These are government bodies that can offer a wide range of advice, help, premises and funds for business.

English Estates. A government-owned property development company, EE builds factory estates in various places, and acts as developer for workshops in rural locations which the Rural Development Commission funds.

Enterprise agencies. These partnerships between the public and private sectors aim to offer advice, help and other facilities to encourage new and existing businesses.

Highlands and Islands Development Board. This is the northern Scottish version of the Rural Development Commission Business Service.

Industrial Training Boards. Although many have been abolished or changed in nature in the last few years, some offer excellent publications to help the new and small firms in their particular industry.

Inland Revenue Inspectors of Taxes. Leaflets and advice are given on the tax position of businesses, which can be most useful to new starters.

Jobcentres. Not only are they a source of recruitment, but Jobcentres also carry a stock of Training Agency (formerly MSC) leaflets and Department of Employment publications, many of which are essential reading for an employer.

Local authorities. They can usually provide information on any industrial aid which may be available locally. In addition, as one of the most influential enforcement bodies acting on small firms, they can advise you on how to avoid trouble. The main contacts are the planning department, health inspectors, fire department, building inspectors and trading standards offices.

Mid-Wales Development. This is another government body which offers help similar to that of the Rural Development Commission's Business Service, but in rural Wales.

Newspaper Publishers Association. This body lays down the rules governing, among other things, mail order advertising in most newspapers and magazines. Anyone planning to sell by this method should contact them well in advance of trying to advertise.

Patent Office. The Patent Office offers an informative set of leaflets on its concerns.

Post Office. The PO gives considerable concessions to volume users of its services in general, and especially to first-time users of direct mail selling. Postal sales representatives at Head Post Offices provide the details.

Rural Development Commission's Business Service (Formerly CoSIRA). This government organisation offers information and advice in depth on all aspects of setting up and running a business. It can deal with technical, management, training and premises matters, as well as giving assistance in raising funds. It operates in English towns and villages of up to 10,000 population, helping firms with up to 20 skilled employees (there is no limit on the number of unskilled).

Tourist Boards. Organised on a regional basis, the Tourist Boards offer management advice, publicity and grants for tourism-based enterprises. These do not have to be just hotels: they are concerned to help most firms having some tourism aspect to their operations. They also publish some useful guides to running different sorts of tourism businesses.

Training Agency (formerly Manpower Services Commission). This body offers courses for new starters, together with living allowances, all paid for by the government. It also gives the Enterprise Allowance for unemployed new starters and the Young Workers Scheme subsidy for employing a young person, and funds the Youth Training Scheme.

Glossary

ACAS. Advisory, Conciliation and Arbitration Service.

accounts. Periodic, at least annual, reports usually consisting of *profit and loss* account and *balance sheet.*

accounting period. Period of time to which a set of accounts refers.

accrual. Allowance in accounts for costs and benefits accrued but not yet realised.

agent. See *sales agent.*

AIDA. The sequence of a sales presentation: Attention, Interest, Desire, Action.

amortisation. Writing off an initial cost over a period of time; see also *depreciation.*

APR. Annual Percentage Rate, ie the true rate of interest.

artwork. Finished design ready for photography, eg for making printing plates.

assets. Property having measurable value.

   current. Debtors plus stock and cash.

   fixed. Plant, equipment, vehicles and buildings.

   liquid. In cash, or easily convertible to cash.

   net. Total assets less liabilities.

   net current. Current assets less current liabilities; also known as working capital.

audit. Independent check and comment on financial records.

authorised capital. The amount of capital which a company is permitted to issue and in what form.

bad debt. Debt that is not recovered.

balance sheet. Statement at a moment in time showing sources and disposition of funds.

bankruptcy. Statutory confiscation of personal assets to settle debts, and prohibition from trading.

base rate. The basic rate of interest above which banks will lend.

bill of exchange. Document unconditionally arranging a future payment.

bill of lading (B/L). Receipt from a ship's master for goods loaded on board.

black economy. The informal part of the economy, usually evading taxation.

bleed. Printing that extends over the entire page and is not surrounded by a 'frame'.

block. A photographically prepared special item for use in *letterpress* printing.

book value. Value of an asset shown in the books, ie after deducting allowances for depreciation; often different from resale value or replacement cost.

BRAD. British Rate and Data: a monthly publication listing advertising media.

break-even. The level of activity at which a firm's profit equals its costs.

broker. A go-between.

budget. A forecast expressed in figures, eg a sales budget, an overheads budget, a cash flow budget.

capital. Total resources invested or available for investment.

capital gain. Rise in the value of an asset.

capital goods. Same as *fixed assets*.

Careers Office. Local authority office charged with finding jobs for young people.

case. The package protecting goods from damage in transit.

cash. Money in readily accessible form, eg in a current account or in banknotes.

cash book. Daily record of cash payments and cash received.

cash flow. The movement of cash into and out of the business as income is received and debts are settled.

channel. Channel of distribution, eg wholesaler – retailer – consumer.

charge. A legally registered right to the proceeds of the disposal of an asset in return for an unpaid debt.

civil law. The system of law relating to private rights, developed by judicial decisions rather than Parliament.

clearing banks. banks of the type familiar to the general public.

closing stock. Stock held at the end of an accounting period.

collateral. Security pledged against borrowing.

condition. Matters in a *contract*, breach of which entitles the offended party to a refund plus damages.

consignment note. Same as *delivery note*.

consignment stock. Stock placed with a distributor and not charged for until sold.

consumer. The end user of a product or service.

consumer goods. Products of the type supplied to the public.

consumer research. Research aimed at identifying the needs, wants and preferences of, and influences on, consumers.

contingency. An item often found in *budgets* – a safety margin.

contract. Binding agreement on two or more parties.

control. Process of identifying and correcting deviations from plan.

co-operative. A business constitution in which the employees own the business: there are many varieties.

copy. Written material for publication.

copy date. The latest date by which a publication can receive material for inclusion.

copyright. Legal protection from copyists automatically applying to any original work, and often signified by a © (date, name).

corporation tax. Tax on the profits of companies.

CoSIRA. Council for Small Industries in Rural Areas – now Rural Development Commission's Business Service.

cost of sales. The cost of goods sold, as shown in profit and loss calculations.

credit. Arrangement for deferring the payment of debts; *also* positive figures in accounts.

credit control. Ensuring that payments due are, as far as possible, received on time.

credit sale. Sale on instalments where ownership passes before payment is complete.

creditor. A person to whom money is owed.

current. Due within one year (in accounting).

debenture. A document recording a charge over the *assets* of a company in return for a loan.

debit. Subtract; *also* negative figures in accounts.

debtor. A person who owes one money.

delivery note. A list of goods delivered on one occasion, usually arriving with the goods themselves.

depreciation. An amount, usually a percentage, by which the using-up of *fixed assets* is expressed as a cost.

direct mail. Sending sales material direct to consumers.

direct response. Selling via advertising which solicits orders and payment direct to the advertiser.

direct selling. Selling direct to the *consumer* outside the normal trade channels.

disciplinary procedure. A defined procedure for dealing with offences by employees.

display. A small advertisement within its own frame.

distress. Legally, to 'levy a distress' is to confiscate goods to enforce payment.

distress purchase. A purchase that has to be made under pressure, usually of time, eg replacement car windscreen.

dividend. Payment to shareholders from a company.

draft. An interim attempt which can be improved upon, eg draft plans; *also* banker's draft: a bank's instructions to pay money from its funds.

E & O E. 'Errors and omissions excepted'; a let-out, sometimes found on invoices.

EFT. Electronic Funds Transfer.

EFTPOS. Electronic Funds transfer at Point of Sale. A system whereby shops can instantly transfer payment from the customer's bank account to their own.

employer's liability insurance. A class of insurance which employers are required to have by law.

endorse. To sign on the back of a cheque, bill etc to transfer its ownership.

equity. That part of a company's funds raised by the sale of shares.

Existing Use Certificate. Written acknowledgement from local authority that a particular use of a building or site is sanctified by the passage of time.

facing matter. Material facing editorial content in a publication.

factor. Wholesaler; *also* one who buys a firm's debts to give it an inflow of cash and obtains settlement of those debts himself.

financial year. Year covered by an annual set of business accounts, not necessarily January to December.

fixed assets. See *assets, fixed.*

fixed capital. Long-term debt, usually shareholders' funds plus long-term loans.

fixed costs. Those costs which do not vary with the level of activity within certain limits, eg rent, rates etc.

franchise. The right to sell a franchisor's products and services.

free issue. A system whereby materials are bought by a firm and issued at no charge to a subcontractor to do work on them.

FRI. Full repairing and insuring (lease).

gearing. Relationship between borrowings and owners' funds in a business (high borrowing and little equity is 'highly geared').

going concern. Assumption that the business is a continuing operation, not about to be liquidated.

goodwill. Difference between the 'going concern' valuation of a business and its book value; a monetary expression of its earning potential over and above its break-up value.

grievance procedure. Defined procedure enabling employees to have employment grievances dealt with.

gross. Full price or total figure before any subtractions are made; *also* serious, as in 'gross misconduct'.

HASAWA. Health and Safety at Work Act.

hire purchase. Payment by instalments where ownership transfers only after payment is complete.

ifc/irc. Inside front cover/inside rear cover.

indemnity. Undertaking to recompense.

inflation accounting. System of accounting which attempts to deal with the effect on financial performance of the changing value of money.

input. Purchase on which VAT is calculated.

insolvency. Inability to pay bills through immediate shortage of cash (could possibly be cleared by realising assets).

inventory. Stock; *also* a list.

invoice. A 'bill' in everyday language.

issued capital. The amount of money raised by a company by the sale of its shares.

joint and several. Together and individual; usually of guarantees etc which can be made by a number of people who are collectively and separately responsible.

letter-head. Writing paper printed with a business name and address.

letterpress. A printing method using pre-formed letters.

LGS. The Government Loan Guarantee Scheme.

liability. Money owed; obligation.

limited company. A legal 'person', separate from its owners, whose liability for its debts is limited to the issued share capital.

lineage. Advertising which is sold by the line, as in typical classified advertisements.

liquid. Having enough cash to meet obligations.

liquidation. Sale of assets and collection of monies owed, to pay off debtors.

liquidity. Ability to meet demands for payment of debts; *also* extent to which a company's assets are in the form of cash or can quickly become cash.

lithography/litho. A method of printing which uses photographically created printing plates.

loan capital. That part of a company's capital raised through loans as opposed to equity and retained profits.

mail order. A method of shopping by post from catalogues.

margin. The profit margin on which a company works. A distributor usually adds a proportion to cost, or expects a percentage of his selling price.

market. A defined public, actually or potentially consumers of goods or a service, or a group of goods or services, eg the leisure market, the baked bean market, the French market.

marketing. The approach to business that starts from the customer's needs and seeks to profit by satisfying them; *also* research, design, distribution, promotion and pricing activities towards that end.

market research. Investigation of the characteristics of a presumed market.

mark-up. The profit that a distributor or shop adds to the cost of an item. Often erroneously used for profit margins in general.

media. Plural of 'medium', frequently used to mean carriers of advertising and information, such as television, radio, newspapers, magazines etc.

Memorandum and Articles of Assocation. The constitution and rules of a company.

merchant banks. Risk investment bodies.

MOPS. Mail Order Protection Scheme.

mortgage. A form of charge, usually over land and premises, but sometimes over chattels, in return for a loan.

net. After subtraction of discounts or wastage; *also* 'payment net' – no discounts given for payment.

net assets. See *assets, net*.

net current assets. See *assets, net current*.

net worth. Total assets less all liabilities.

news release. Same as *press release*.

NPA. Newspaper Publishers Association.

off the page. Same as *direct response*.

opening stock. Stock held at the beginning of an accounting period.

operating profit. Gross profit less overheads; excludes cost of finance, tax etc.

operating statement. Document showing gross sales, *cost of sales*, gross profit, *overheads* and net profit before tax and interest.

outer. The outer transit case holding, say, a dozen packs of a product.

output. Sales on which VAT is calculated.

overdraft. A loan on current account which may fluctuate with day-to-day transactions up to a defined limit, and may be recalled at a moment's notice.

overheads. General costs which cannot be accurately attributed to individual products, eg rent, telephone, insurance etc.

overtrading. Having difficulty with *liquidity* due to a level of sales greater than the capital base can support.

P&L. Profit and Loss. Calculation of profit over a past period of time; or in *budget*, expected in the future.

Pareto's Law. 80 per cent of activity produces 20 per cent of results, and vice versa.

partnership. Business constitution in which each partner is personally responsible for the entire liabilities and obligations of the business.

party plan. A method of selling to parties of people at the home of one of them.

passing off. Pretence that goods were made by other than their true manufacturer.

patent. An expensive but powerful legal protection for an original technological invention.

PAYE. Pay As You Earn; usually deduction of income tax and National Insurance made by the employer from employee's gross pay.

plant. Equipment, machines.

plc. Public limited company.

pos/pop. Point of sale/point of purchase; the place where sale or purchase occurs.

preferential creditor. Creditor with a right to be paid before unsecured creditors; includes the Government, employees etc.

presentation. An explanatory and persuasive address to an audience, usually involving visual aids.

press release. A news story, written by or on behalf of its subject, and circulated to the news media in the hope of publication.

profit and loss. See P&L.

pro-forma. Documents sent in advance of transaction, eg a pro-forma invoice is one which will be paid before goods are despatched, or will alert a customer (particularly overseas) to the full cost of the consignment; *also* a standard document or letter fulfilling statutory requirements, eg the statement of terms and conditions to employees.

profit margin. See *margin*.

proof. An example of printing for checking and approval before the main print run is started.

PR/public relations. Activity designed to influence public opinion favourably.

QA. Quality assurance.

quality circles. A system whereby all employees contribute to management consideration of quality affairs and problem-solving.

QC. Quality control.

R&D. Research and development.

rate card. Price-list for advertising.

receiver. Person appointed by a court to take control of and protect the assets of a company which is unable to meet its obligations.

redundancy. The disappearance of a job causing dismissal or transfer of an employee; *also* intentional over-specification to reduce risk of failure.

registered design. An original design protected by registration; this gives better security than copyright.

registered office. The office of a company registered with the Registrar of Companies. Often it is the office of a professional adviser to the firm.

registered trade mark. A trade name or mark protected by registration.

registration number. The number allocated on registration of a company by the Registrar of Companies.

reservation of title. Retention of ownership of goods until (usually) they have been paid for.

retained profits. Profits that have not been distributed to shareholders as *dividends.*

revaluation. Valuing existing assets on present-day criteria.

Romalpa. A legal case affecting rights to reservation of title.

rop. Run of paper (in advertising); placed where it suits the publisher.

sales agent. A person who obtains orders in return for commission.

sales promotion. Activity which motivates desired purchasing patterns.

scc. Single-column centimetre (in advertising).

Schedule D. Income tax regime for the self-employed.

Schedule E. Income tax regime for employed people.

segment. A defined portion of a *market.*

segmentation. The process of dividing a *market* into notional portions.

self-employed. Working on own account while supplying tools and equipment, and for hours which are self-determined.

semi-display. Advertising which rules off one advertisement from its neighbours in a column.

settlement discount. Discount for paying debt within a time limit.

share capital. Funds invested in a *limited company* in return for shares.

small claims procedure. Informal procedure for recovering debts of up to £2000 via county courts.

sale trader. A self-employed person trading on his own responsibility.

solvent. Having enough cash to pay bills.

sor/sale or return. Arrangement whereby distributor pays only for stock that he sells.

SSP/Statutory Sick Pay. Employer pays sick employee and reclaims from government.

statement. A summary of transactions on an account.

statute. Act of Parliament.

stay. Delay.

stock. Raw materials, work in progress, and finished goods.

structure plan. Local authority plan delineating town and country planning policies.

suspension. Requiring an employee not to report to work, but without dismissing him; normally, suspension on full pay.

SWOT. An analysis of a company's internal Strengths and Weaknesses, and external Opportunities and Threats.

tangible asset. Asset that can be touched, eg machine, but not goodwill.

tender. A fixed-price offer to sell or buy, typically used by public authorities' purchasing departments.

term loan. A loan repayable over a fixed period of time.

terms and conditions. Conditions under which commitments are accepted.

trade description. Description of goods or services; by law, it must be true.

Trading Standards Department. Local authority department responsible for enforcement of much consumer-protection legislation.

title. Ownership; see *reservation of title*.

tort. A civil wrong; see *civil law*.

tribunal. Industrial Tribunal appointed to hear cases of misconduct in employment matters alleged by current or former employees.

Truck Acts. Acts of Parliament mainly requiring wages to be paid in cash.

unsecured creditor. One with no security for his debt other than a promise to pay.

value. A perception based on a combination of price and expected or actual performance.

value added. The difference between the cost of materials and their sales value in processed form.

variable costs. Costs which vary with the level of activity, eg materials consumed.

VAT. Value Added Tax; a sales tax.

visual aid. Graphic or other tangible aid to explanation.

Wages Council. Statutory body which sets minimum wages for employees in a low-paid industry.

warranty. A term in a contract, breach of which entitles the aggrieved person to a refund.

Willing's Press Guide. A directory of publications.

winding-up. Closing down a business, selling assets, settling debts, and distributing any residue among its owners.

working capital. Funds used to finance day-to-day dealings; formally defined as *net current assets* (current assets less current liabilities).

work in progress. Part-finished goods in the production process.

writing-down allowance. Same as *depreciation.*

written statement. Written confirmation of the terms of an employment contract.

YTS. Youth Training Scheme; government scheme intended to give training and work experience to young people.

Further Reading from Kogan Page

Be Your Own PR Man, 2nd edition, Michael Bland
Be Your Own Company Secretary, A J Scrine
The Business Guide to Effective Speaking, Jacqueline Dunckel and Elizabeth
   Parnham
Business Rip-Offs and How to Avoid Them, Tony Attwood
Buying and Renovating Houses for Profit, 2nd edition, Kim Ludman and R
   D Buchanan
Buying a Shop, 3rd edition, A St John Price
Buying for Business Tony Attwood
Debt Collection Made Easy, Peter Buckland
Direct Mail: Principles and Practice, Robin Fairlie
Export for the Small Business, 2nd edition, Henry Deschampsneufs
Financial Management for the Small Business, 2nd edition, Colin Barrow
Getting Sales, Richard D Smith and Ginger Dick
The Guardian Guide to Running a Small Business, 7th edition, ed Clive
   Woodcock
How to Advertise, Kenneth Roman and Jane Maas
How to Be An Even Better Manager, Michael Armstrong
How to Buy a Business, 2nd edition, Peter Farrell
How to Cut Your Business Costs, Peter D Brunt
How to Prepare a Business Plan, Edward Blackwell
Importing for the Small Business, 2nd edition, Mag Morris
Law for the Small Business, 6th edition, Patricia Clayton
Raising Finance: The Guardian Guide for the Small Business, 3rd edition, Clive
   Woodcock
Running Your Own Antiques Business, Noël Riley and Godfrey Golzen
Running Your Own Boarding Kennels, Sheila Zabawa
Running Your Own Building Business, Kim Ludman
Running Your Own Catering Business, Ursula Garner and Judy Ridgway
Running Your Own Driving School, Nigel Stacey
Running Your Own Hairdressing Salon, Christine Harvey and Helen
   Steadman
Running Your Own Mail Order Business, Malcolm Breckman
Running Your Own Photographic Business, John Rose and Linda Hankin
Running Your Own Pub, Elven Money
Running Your Own Restaurant, Diane Hughes and Godfrey Golzen

STARTING A SUCCESSFUL SMALL BUSINESS

Running Your Own Shop, Roger Cox
Running Your Own Small Hotel, Joy Lennick
Running Your Own Typing Service, Doreen Huntley
Running Your Own Wine Bar, Judy Ridgway
The Stoy Hayward Business Tax Guide (annual)
Successful Expansion for the Small Business, M J Morris
Successful Marketing for the Small Business, 2nd edition, Dave Patten
Taking up a Franchise, 5th edition, Colin Barrow and Godfrey Golzen
Which Business? How to Select the Right Opportunity for Starting Up, Stephen Halliday

Index